261.83229

use and misuse

use and misuse

a christian perspective on drugs

ollie batchelor

Inter-Varsity Press

INTER-VARSITY PRESS
38 De Montfort Street, Leicester LE1 7GP, England

First published 1999

British Library Cataloguing in Publication Data
A catalogue record for this book is available from the British Library.

ISBN 0–85111–599–3

Set in Garamond
Typeset in Great Britain
Printed in Great Britain by Caledonian International Book
Manufacturing Ltd, Glasgow.

*Inter-Varsity Press is the book-publishing division of the Universities and
Colleges Christian Fellowship (formerly the Inter-Varsity Fellowship), a student
movement linking Christian Unions in universities and colleges in the United
Kingdom, and a member movement of the International Fellowship of
Evangelical Students. For information about local and national activities write
to UCCF, 38 De Montfort Street, Leicester LE1 7GP.*

contents

acknowledgments

Authors' acknowledgments can easily seem both self-effacing and trite. Having experienced the struggle of writing this book, so different from the heady days of its inception, I have become genuinely conscious not only of my shortcomings and deficiencies, but of a sincere debt of gratitude I owe to many others.

In particular I would like to express my thanks to my parents, for years of support, understanding and faithful encouragement; Gregory SSF and all the brothers at Alnmouth Friary for providing a safe and peaceful place to reflect, receive and renew my energies; Pauline Shelton for always being available to offer advice and comments that got me through a great many sticking points; All Souls Langham Place and Greenbelt Arts Festival for shaping so much of my thinking over many years; Dave Cave for his excellent essay *A Biblical Theology of Addiction* which helped me as a lay person to grasp some of the important theological issues and inspired me to widen the field of application; and the hundreds of people with drug and alcohol problems with whom I have been involved and who have given of themselves with great generosity in spite of their need. In particular I would like to recall Colleen, Jackie, Gary, Kerry, Steve and Chiny, whose untimely deaths taught me so much. I would also like to thank the Revds Caroline Dick and Geoff Miller and the Durham Diocesan Board of Social Responsibility for their helpful comments and encouragement and for their willingness to engage with this subject; the numerous agencies, organizations and churches who provided me with information and ideas about their involvement in this field (apologies to any schemes and initiatives disappointed not to have been contacted, mentioned or included); Inter-Varsity Press; and Jen, for her love, support and understanding, particularly during the times of struggle, who throughout was painfully aware that I was spending far more of my waking hours with my PC than with her.

To all of these people and to many others not mentioned I would like to express my gratitude.

Quotations at the head of each chapter are from *Alice's Adventures in Wonderland* by Lewis Carroll.

introduction

Drug use is everybody's problem. The issue of the use and misuse of alcohol affects and always has affected every one of us. Because it is easily available and widely used by all sections of society, one drinker in twenty-five is thought to be addicted to the drug.[1] What is true of alcohol is increasingly true of illicit drugs. A range of different substances is relatively easily obtained, and use of these drugs is now widespread, particularly among people under the age of thirty.

As Christians, we are not exempt. Research conducted at that most Christian setting of all, Spring Harvest, revealed that a quarter of twelve- to sixteen-year-olds and more than half of those over seventeen had been offered or had tried illegal drugs. Around 12% of twelve- to sixteen-year-olds and 52% of those over seventeen were drinking alcohol weekly.[2]

This book endeavours to look at the realities of current drug use and considers some of the implications and issues for Christians. It is hoped that it will stimulate the growing Christian reflection about drugs and help towards eliminating the subject imbalance on the shelves of Christian bookstores. Over the last ten years I have waited in vain for somebody else to write it. Finally, with some trepidation I have undertaken the task myself in the hope that it will help to open up the discussion and take forward both individual and corporate Christian responses to drug and alcohol use.

Although I have worked in the field of substance misuse for many years and have accrued considerable knowledge about drugs and alcohol and their use, I make no claim to be a theologian. In the words of John Stott, who has done so much to help Christians think through contemporary social issues, 'what I am venturing to offer the public is not a polished [theological piece], but the rough-hewn work of an ordinary Christian who is struggling to think Christianly, that is, apply the biblical revelation to the pressing issues of the day'.[3] To do this I have engaged in the process which Dr Stott has termed 'double listening'.[4] Double listening is our Christian calling to live under the Word of God while living in the world. In the context of drugs, this means that we must listen to what the world is saying about the realities and facts about drugs, and balance this against the Bible, the Word of God. The resulting synthesis offers a distinctly Christian perspective on drugs. My hope is that it will help Christians of all ages and circumstances, as well as churches, both large and small, to think about the issue of drugs from a biblical standpoint and take an authentic Christian stance. Through this, the church may at last find a place at the centre of both the public debate and the action.

drugs <u>and</u> society

chapter

one

a world of drugs

The White Rabbit put on his spectacles. 'Where
shall I begin, please your Majesty?' he asked.
'Begin at the beginning,' the King said, gravely.

We live on a drug-taking planet. Whether it is in the suburbs
of Sydney, the Yorkshire Dales, the Amazon rainforests or
the Lower East Side of New York, the use of mind- and
mood-altering substances is part of everyday life for the
majority of people. They use many different kinds of drugs,
and they use them in many different ways, but the reason for
their popularity is unchanged by distance, location or by the
coming and going of millennia. Human beings have a deep
desire to alter and control the way they think, feel and act.
Drugs do this for us quickly and easily.

Ancient habits

Drug use is as old as civilization. There is evidence of the use
of alcohol, opium, cocaine and cannabis as far back as we can
trace. The fermentation of alcohol is a natural process, and
psychoactive plants and herbs grow in most parts of the
world. Early tribes and societies used them medicinally,
incorporated them into religious ceremonies and rituals or
took them for social and recreational purposes. The coming
of the major world religions did little to stop the use of

13

drugs; indeed, legends attribute the discovery of opium to the Buddha and coffee to Muhammad.[1]

Most cultures also had rules forbidding the use of certain substances, and what is acceptable changes over time. Laudanum, opium and cocaine were widely accepted in British society until the early twentieth century. Queen Victoria, John Keats, Sigmund Freud and Sir Walter Scott were just a few of the regular users of cocaine and opium. Even among the Christian greats, William Wilberforce was a regular user of opium, while Martin Luther had been a competitive drinker and Charles Spurgeon had a strong liking for cigars and ale. Yesterday's acceptable drug has, in many cases, become today's controlled substance.

Across different cultures the variations between what is acceptable and what is controlled are even more confusing. Alcohol, so widely accepted in western society, is condemned and prohibited in Muslim countries, while cannabis is often tolerated. Cocaine, the target of many American anti-drug measures, was the crucial ingredient that for twenty years helped to make that quintessential American product, Coca-Cola, the real thing. It was replaced by caffeine in 1904. Meanwhile, in some South American countries, coca leaves are packaged into little perforated bags, which, after being doused in hot water, give a weak cocaine 'tea', not far removed from the British cuppa. Although increasingly frowned upon, tobacco is still almost universally permitted, but it was once dealt with in Switzerland by the pillory, in Persia by suffocation from smoke and in Russia by flogging, castration and slitting the user's lips.

The reasons for such variations are usually mixed. A society's traditions, values and religious beliefs, as well as the interests of those in power, are all significant. Potential harm is also a determinant, but the personal, social and economic problems caused by a substance are not always reflected in a society's attitude towards it. Alcohol has brought untold human misery in its wake, yet its long tradition of use, its widespread acceptability among all levels of western society and the massive vested interests of manufacturers make it unlikely that any serious attempt will be made to outlaw it, or even to tighten existing controls.

Controls of some sort are important, even for acceptable substances, and, in almost all societies, mood-altering drugs are controlled to a greater or lesser extent. In the UK, financial controls such as taxation were introduced centuries before more specific legislative control measures. In 1908, the sale of opium was restricted to those people known to the chemist; supply of cocaine, morphine and heroin was controlled in 1917, alcohol during the First World War and cannabis in 1925. Throughout the next thirty years, alcohol began to recover from the decline caused by the temperance movement, tobacco-smoking strengthened its stranglehold, and the military explored the potential of drugs in warfare, either to improve the performance of their own troops or to impair that of the enemy. By the 1960s, as youth culture exploded into view, drug use became increasingly widespread and was believed to be a growing problem for society. Laws were passed over the course of several years, controlling the prescribing, supply and use of drugs such as amphetamine, LSD and heroin. In 1971 the Misuse of Drugs Act consolidated the earlier mishmash of legislation, and this Act, together with the 1968 Medicines Act and the more recent 1985 Intoxicating Substances Act, accounts for the UK controls on most drugs that can be misused.

Although drug-taking has long been an established part of all human societies, ease of travel and the growth in technology mean that now a greater variety of drugs is more widely available than ever before. Whether the latest is a little-known plant from equatorial South America or a designer drug made in a state-of-the-art laboratory, the choice is constantly expanding. The producers of both legal and illegal substances are now invariably large-scale commercial operations, and the inability to advertise illegal or pharmaceutical products publicly is scarcely a hindrance to their sales because the market is so demand-led. The formula is simple. We want to think or feel differently, and we know that drugs can do this for us by changing our moods to make us feel better. We therefore demand a drug that will provide us with the feelings we want, and we (usually) manage to obtain it, because suppliers are in business to meet our demand. In the world of the market, moral questions about the rights and wrongs of drugs easily become an irrelevance. Controlled substances will always be available because there is both a supply and a demand. Controls such as licensing of premises, prescriptions, age requirements and legislation can at best only curb the extent of their use.

A confused picture

In Britain, public concern about drug use has increased since the late 1980s, focusing on young people in particular, since they are thought to be most at risk. Over recent years, their alleged use of Ecstasy, alcopops, aerosols and heroin has at different times been at the centre of a media-led moral panic about drugs. 'Lost to drugs', 'The war in the playground', 'Evil dealer goes free', 'Killer drug', are typical of the newspaper headlines that bombard us. When the story dies down, the adult population, which feels largely ignorant about drugs, is left with distorted impressions and ideas about the nature and use of these substances. Fear and ignorance predominate, capitalized upon by political opportunists of all parties. In the middle of it all, young people look on. Many regard the attitudes and behaviour of government and the adult population as flawed, or at least full of double standards and hypocrisy. The picture is both confused and confusing.

The increasing amount and quality of drugs research in the UK are beginning to combat some of this tangle, helping to build up a more accurate picture of what is happening. There is now a mass of statistics and information about drugs and alcohol, ranging from the prevalence, patterns and explanations of use to the effectiveness (and ineffectiveness) of prevention and treatment. The results confirm that, over recent years at least, illegal drug use has been increasing, particularly among young people. At the same time, the age at which young people are first using drugs has gone down. There is little question that the availability of illegal drugs is becoming a normal part of life for most young people, although use of illegal drugs is still restricted to a minority, albeit a sizeable one. Around 45% of sixteen- to twenty-nine-year olds admit to having tried illegal drugs at some point in their lives, but only 15% had used them during the previous month.[2] Among young people of school age, between a quarter and a third of fourteen- to fifteen-year-olds say that they have tried illegal drugs, while 5% of twelve- to thirteen-year-olds say they have done so.[3] But the increase in drug use is a trend not just among young people; 28% of those between sixteen and fifty-nine years of age have also used illegal drugs.[4] Within all of these age groups, cannabis is by far the most commonly used illegal substance.

Drug use is not just about illegal substances. Alcohol is currently experiencing a fashionable renaissance, led by premium lagers, white ciders and alcopops. While 4% more people are choosing to be alcohol-free than was the case in the mid-1980s, those who do drink are consuming more. Alcohol consumption in 1996 was higher than in any of the previous ten years. UK expenditure exceeded £28,000 million, which is more than is spent on clothing and around half of what is spent on food. More than a quarter of men exceed the maximum recommended male intake of twenty-one units[5] of alcohol per week, while 14% of women drink more than their maximum recommended level of fourteen units per week.[6]

Most drug-related deaths in Britain result from cigarette-smoking – around 110,000 a year, or 0.9% of the smoking population. This compares with an annual death rate of around 0.0002% of Ecstasy users and 1.5% of heroin users.[7] In spite of such statistics and the health warnings, lawsuits, high taxation and adverse publicity to which smoking gives rise, it continues to hold its own among young people. Though it is not legal for those under sixteen years of age to buy cigarettes, nearly 10% of eleven- to fifteen-year-olds smoke regularly. They consume an estimated one billion cigarettes, costing something in the order of £120 million. Among the adult population the number of cigarette-smokers has steadily declined since the late 1970s, yet a quarter of all adults are still regular smokers. Total UK expenditure on cigarettes is nearly £12,000 million a year.[8]

The prescribing of mood-altering tablets and medicine by doctors remains high. In 1996, spending on antidepressants increased by 30%.[9] Included in this massive rise were over 5.5 million prescriptions for Prozac, given out to around half a million people, some as young as eight years old.[10] Prescription drugs include tranquillizers such as temazepam and Valium, which, despite their heinous track record, remain a seemingly simple quick fix for desperate patients and hard-pressed doctors alike. Most recent figures suggest that every year 5% of men and 12% of women use tranquillizers for at least a month.[11] Many of these tranquillizers and painkillers have crossed the gap from doctors' surgeries to street-corner deals, where a Valium tablet costs as little as 50 pence, making a handful a cheaper and increasingly popular knock-out alternative to alcohol.

The pattern is the same in Europe and the rest of the world. In the case of tobacco, China has 200 million smokers, tobacco sales in Africa increased by 33% between 1970 and 1980, and the Far East is now the target of the major American and British tobacco companies. Europe produces over half the world's supply of alcohol, with the French topping the league for consumption with an annual individual consumption rate of 12.4 litres of pure alcohol (approximately 22 pints). The UK comes in at number twenty, behind countries such as Hungary, Germany and Australia. In the United States, cocaine use peaked at six million regular users in the mid-1980s, while in Colombia, one of the world's biggest cocaine producers, the level of solvent use among street children and homeless youngsters has reached epidemic proportions. In Guatemala it is estimated that 90% of rough sleepers are dependent upon paint thinner and cheap glue. In the USA, an estimated 6% of the population are regular illicit drug users, while for those between twelve and seventeen years this figure rises to 9%. Availability of drugs is regarded as a normal part of life for many young Americans, with 15% of twelve- to seventeen-year-olds having been approached in the previous month by someone selling drugs.[12]

A part of culture

The use of drugs and alcohol is an intrinsic part of our culture. Every day on our televisions, films, soaps, comedy and drama programmes give out countless subtle messages about alcohol that reinforce its use and acceptability. Films and documentaries on drug-running, drug hoists, police raids and drug subcultures invariably establish drugs as exciting and glamorous. The days of cigarette advertising may now be numbered, but for many people connections have already been made. The association between smoking and a cool, calm and sophisticated image will stay with them for life.

Sport too is inextricably linked with drug use. Sports sponsorship has been a popular form of advertising for decades. Trophies in a range of sports have been named after alcohol and tobacco manufacturers or their products. Snooker and Formula One motor-racing have received substantial backing from tobacco companies for many years, while football, cricket and rugby teams have the names and logos of breweries emblazoned across their shirts. Tobacco advertising in sport will be banned throughout the UK by 2003 in all but Formula One motor-racing, but alcohol advertising has no such problems. In 1997, drinks companies accounted for 163 out of 995 sports sponsorship deals, worth a total of £321.6 million.[13]

The other side of drugs in sport is their use to improve performance. Stories about drug use by athletes, cyclists, swimmers and many other sports people make headline news with alarming regularity. The substances may be more sophisticated, but the idea is nothing new; Greek Olympians ate large quantities of sheeps' testicles, believed to improve their performance in the Games. The problematic use of 'recreational' drugs by sports stars is also becoming more apparent, though alcohol undoubtedly remains the most widely misused within the British sporting scene.

Music has long been associated with drugs and alcohol, and the industry has had its fair share of casualties too. Discussion about whether music was written under the influence of drugs or whether the lyrics encourage young people to take drugs is perennial among media and politicians. What is clear is that musicians are merely following the long tradition of poets, writers and artists who used substances to provide inspiration for their work or to escape from the pain of their existence.

Here to stay

Drugs, then, are part and parcel of our lives. The use of legal and prescribed drugs is deeply entrenched within our society and our individual minds. We want a quick fix. Illegal substances are also here to stay, and, for many people, the gap between illegal and legal drugs is becoming increasingly blurred. So welcome to the pick 'n' mix drugstore of life.

two

the name of the game

> 'Speak English!' said the Eaglet. 'I don't know
> the meaning of half those long words, and,
> what's more, I don't believe you do either!' And
> the Eaglet bent down its head to hide a smile:
> some of the other birds tittered audibly.

In a recently published dictionary of prison slang, the compilers found that their biggest problem was keeping track of the names and meanings of drugs and drug-related activities. The language of the drugs world changes regularly, old and traditional terms being replaced by new and fashionable ones, as the ever-shifting culture invents and redefines itself. There are two main reasons for this changing terminology, both of which establish those people not in the know as outsiders.

First, it helps to keep activities under cover, which is understandable given the illegality of much drug use and the social disapproval that generally surrounds it. Secondly, there is a very close association between drugs and youth culture, where words and language are constantly evolving or being changed. This is true of fashion, music and other consumer goods just as much as of drugs. Old commodities are marketed anew, either to make them appear new or to provide variations on their previous shape or form.

The introduction of alcopops in 1995–6 was an example

reference

of a deliberate and concerted campaign by the drinks industry to manufacture and market products that would appeal to young people.[1] Despite media speculation and subsequent public concern that alcopops were intended to appeal to those in their early teens, there is far more reason to believe that they were actually targeted at older teenage and early twenties nightclubbers, who had given up alcohol in favour of Ecstasy and cannabis, washed down with a glass of mineral water.

Another example of marketing in the drug world is provided by a piece of research into a large-scale heroin outbreak. This showed that increased use of the drug did not just happen of its own accord but arose as a result of excess supplies of the drug being marketed in a form and at a price that were attractive to young users. Thus the drug was widely referred to as 'brown' rather than 'heroin', and emphasis was placed upon the fact that it could be smoked, in order to dissipate the fears and stigma attached to injecting drugs.[2]

LSD is another good example of re-packaging. Following a resurgence in its use in the 1980s, LSD has managed to remain more or less permanently up to date, because the pictures used on the impregnated paper squares are constantly changed to feature contemporary images of local, national or international significance.[3]

The changing language and culture of the streets are mirrored by the changing terminology within the professional drug field. Here, definitions and concepts relating to substance use are changed, refined and developed as tools to describe and make sense of the behaviour. Digging deeper to establish the meanings of some of these words and concepts is therefore an essential step on our road to understanding.

What is a drug?

Even defining the term 'drug' is fraught with difficulty. The term is imprecise and means different things to different people. For some it relates to the range of pharmaceutical products that are manufactured: 'They've discovered a new miracle drug.' Others see it as referring to substances that are addictive ('He's on drugs'), or as substances that are illegal, as in 'the war on drugs'. The World Health Organization says that a drug is 'any substance that when taken into the body may modify one or more of its functions'.[4] On the basis of this, aspirin, sugar and antihistamines are drugs just as much as heroin and cocaine. Accurate as this definition may be, it is far too broad to be of help in the present discussion. In looking at drug use and misuse, our focus is on those substances that have psychological or psychoactive effects upon users, changing the way they think, feel or behave. This excludes the thousands of drugs used to treat physical ailments and disease that have no direct influence on the patient's mind. Focusing on psychoactive substances also makes a definition easier. The term 'drug' will therefore be taken to mean any chemical substance, whether of natural or synthetic origin, which can be used to alter perception, mood or other psychological state.[5]

The right words

On the basis of this definition, substances such as alcohol, coffee, tobacco, solvents and tranquillizers are just as much drugs as those that are illegal, since they all alter perception, mood and behaviour. 'Drugs' is therefore a blanket term covering a range of substances including the socially acceptable ones. The phrase 'drugs and alcohol' is sometimes used to emphasize the inclusion of alcohol, and the term 'substances' is also used as an all-inclusive term covering illicit drugs together with alcohol, tobacco and solvents. In this book the terms 'drugs', 'substances' and 'drugs and alcohol' will be used interchangeably.

Another area of confusion lies with the terms 'use', 'misuse' and 'abuse'. Generally speaking, the first two are used in preference to 'abuse'. Thus one talks of 'drug use' or 'substance use' to refer to the intake of any drugs, while 'drug misuse' or 'substance misuse' is used to mean drug or substance use that is physically and/or psychologically harmful. Such clear definitions minimize the tendency for these terms to be value-laden. A student recently wrote to say

reference

that she and her friends used alcohol regularly, but she was shocked to have discovered that in doing so they also misused an illegal drug. This betrayed her view that alcohol was an acceptable substance, whereas illegal drug-taking was unacceptable and must automatically constitute misuse. On closer investigation, if 'misuse' of a substance meant that it was causing harm, the students' high level of alcohol consumption may well have fallen into this category. While care is therefore needed in referring to use and misuse, the term 'drug abuse' is best avoided completely, because it is so morally loaded and has unhelpful connotations.[6]

A helpful way of understanding drug use divides it into three forms: experimental, recreational and problematic use. 'Experimental drug use' means exactly what it says. This often takes place within a group where an individual tries a drug to see what it is like. Most of us can identify with this, from trying tea or coffee as a child, or our first cigarette or alcoholic drink. If we don't enjoy the experience or effects, we may not use it again, or at least may be deterred from using it for a while. If we like it and decide to continue using the drug, it is known as 'recreational drug use'. This is drinking or drug-taking as a 'pastime' – often a social activity that has become part of a person's lifestyle. In the UK, caffeine and alcohol are the most widely used recreational drugs. In some Muslim countries, where alcohol is frowned upon, caffeine and cannabis are more acceptable recreational drugs. The key to this category is not so much what the substance is but the pattern of its use – any drug can be used recreationally, even substances such as cocaine or heroin.

The final category, 'problematic drug use', is what was referred to earlier as 'drug misuse'. Here people begin to develop problems as a result of their drug-taking. These problems could be any one or a combination of social, psychological, physical, legal or economic factors. Individuals tend not to notice the onset of difficulties themselves, or else deny and minimize their significance.

'I didn't like the look of her,' one mother explained. 'I thought she was beginning to look very strained and white and she was losing a lot of weight. Things around the house were going missing too. Eventually I asked her what was wrong. I even asked her if she was using drugs, but was met with denial. It sounds stupid now that I know what it was, but at the time I just felt relieved, you know, that she had said it wasn't drugs.'

Many problem drug-users are dependent on their drug(s) of choice. 'Dependent drug use' is more popularly referred to as 'addiction', though this, together with the term 'addict', is sometimes avoided because it carries too many negative associations and stereotypes as well as implying a loss of volition. 'Dependency' exists if a person has a compulsion to continue to use a substance in order to remain physically well or psychologically able to function. As one person put it: 'I need my heroin every day not to get high but to feel normal, like everyone else.' Only some drugs create a physical dependence such that if a person stops using it, he or she experiences physical pains, shakes and illnesses. Heroin with its cold turkey, and alcohol with its DTs, are examples of this. In contrast, all substances can lead to a psychological dependency whereby the user depends upon the drug emotionally and mentally to get by.

Although people move between the categories of experimentation, recreational use and problematic use, there is no automatic route between them. For example, not everyone who experiments with alcohol becomes a recreational drinker, and, of those who are recreational drinkers, only a small percentage will become problem or dependent drinkers. It is true, however, that recreational users have previously been experimenters, while dependent users were almost certainly recreational users at one stage. The important point to make is that movement between these categories is not automatic for any drug, but the danger lies in the fact that this is always a possibility. All recreational users believe that they are in control of their use, which may be true for the majority; but some gradually use their substance of choice more and more frequently, and, without noticing it, start to lose control. This marks the movement from recreational to dependent drug use.

A variation on this theme is the 'escalation theory', which

argues that individuals using one substance will automatically move on to a more dangerous substance. This is most often expressed as a fear that someone using cannabis will progress to heroin. Heroin users may even be produced to bear witness to the fact that they used cannabis first of all. This is not in dispute, but there is no evidence of automatic escalation and progression between drugs, a conclusion reached by both government inquiries and research.[7] Believing in the idea of escalation because we would like it to be true, because it seems logical or because people with serious drug problems have generally used a wide range of drugs does not make it true. Most people with heroin or cocaine problems have all used cannabis previously, but those who try cannabis have almost all used tobacco and alcohol previously too. Nobody would suggest that the use of alcohol automatically leads to using cannabis.

The fact that cannabis is obtained illegally does mean that users are likely to come into contact with those who supply other illegal drugs, increasing the chance of their trying these other substances. It is also true that many of those using cannabis are interested in changing the way they feel and experience life and this too may increase the likelihood that they will take other drugs. Nevertheless, progression is neither automatic nor inevitable, and the escalation theory is therefore not only a misrepresentation but also unhelpful. For example, parents who discover that their son or daughter is using cannabis assume that there will be a domino effect ending in chaotic heroin misuse. This false belief and the fear it generates can fuel any existing communication difficulties between the parent(s) and young person, leading to an entrenchment in their respective positions and at the very least an increased risk of greater drug involvement.

Terms to avoid

As already mentioned, there are some terms, such as 'abuse', that are best avoided because they mislead or have negative associations in many people's minds. The terms 'hard drugs' and 'soft drugs' are also best avoided, since this creates an artificial division, implying that one group of drugs is dangerous while another group is safer and therefore less of a concern. 'Thank goodness Chris has been using only soft drugs' may not amount to explicit approval for what Chris has been doing, but it does carry the implication that it is relatively OK. That is certainly how Chris is likely to interpret it. Apart from giving this wrong impression, the picture is far more complex than a simple 'soft' and 'hard' distinction suggests. While some substances certainly do have a greater potential for harm than others, it is not just the drug, but its strength, the way it is taken and the frequency of use that influence harm and risk. People can have problems from so-called soft drugs because all drugs can create psychological dependency. Chris may be using *only* 'soft drugs', but he could still have a lot of problems as a result.

A common language?

It is important to use the right words and understand what they mean. This is not about being fashionable, playing down a problem or being politically correct, nor is it an attempt to make the unpalatable appear more acceptable. Sorting out our terminology is a bit like clearing a building site of rubble. It is an essential starting-point. If this discussion of terminology has aided our understanding and helped us to avoid using terms that label and stigmatize, we have not only cleared the building site of rubble but have begun to lay good foundations for the building work that follows.

reference

chapter

three

drugs and their effects

> Soon her eyes fell on a little glass box that was
> lying under the table: she opened it, and found
> in it a very small cake, on which the words 'EAT
> ME' were beautifully marked in currants. 'Well,
> I'll eat it,' said Alice, 'and if it makes me grow
> larger, I can reach the key; and if it makes me
> grow smaller, I can creep under the door; so
> either way I'll get into the garden!'

Drugs come in all shapes and sizes. Some grow naturally and can be used in their original form (magic mushrooms, cannabis, tobacco); some are extracted from plants (opium, caffeine, cocaine, heroin); while others are made in laboratories as part of a chemical process (LSD, alcohol, Ecstasy, solvents, nitrites, tranquillizers, etc). Although every drug has its own particular effects, several other factors influence both the effects and the risks involved in using different drugs.

Amount and strength. These qualities are easier to perceive with legal drugs because strength and purity are standardized. We don't buy a bottle of alcohol, but alcoholic drinks whose differing strengths are marked on the bottle or pump. Prescribed drugs, too, come in standard doses. Thus we know what we are getting. With illegal drugs it is harder to tell, because there is no check on purity or strength. Cannabis can vary a great deal in its strength, and powdered drugs

reference

29

such as amphetamine, cocaine and heroin are often cut or mixed with other things by the supplier so that the drug will go further. Amphetamine is generally as low as 5%–20% purity, while heroin is often between 30% and 50% purity.[1] Non-powder drugs such as LSD, Ecstasy and steroids also vary depending on where they were made. With illegal drugs, buyers never know exactly what or how much they are getting for their money.

How drugs are taken. The way in which drugs are taken determines how quickly the effects are felt, the intensity of these effects and the associated risks. When taking any drug, the aim is to get the substance into the bloodstream so that it reaches the brain and produces the desired effect. There are four main ways of doing this.

1. Orally. The drug is swallowed and absorbed by the stomach and small intestine and from there enters the bloodstream. This is a slow process with the effect coming on gradually. The majority of drugs can be taken in this way, but with a few drugs, such as heroin or cocaine, it is either ineffective or inefficient.

2. By inhalation. The drug is inhaled into the lungs and from there it passes to the bloodstream. This method gives a rapid effect, but again can be used only with certain drugs. They must be in the form of either a gas or a fine spray such as solvents or amyl nitrate, or in smoke particles, as with nicotine, cannabis, heroin and crack.

3. Across the mucous membranes. Here the drug passes across the moist surfaces or linings of the mouth, nose, throat, eyes or rectum into the tiny capillaries and blood vessels and so into the main bloodstream. This method is used when sniffing cocaine, amphetamine or snuff, but a similar principle is involved when some painkilling tablets are dissolved under the tongue. To be taken in this way the drugs must be fat-soluble.

4. Injection. Almost any non-gaseous drug can be injected, and often is. Some drugs are soluble and more suitable for injection, but powders can be mixed with citric or acetic acid and heated to dissolve them, while tablets can be crushed and at least partially dissolved to allow injection.

This may be done under the skin (known as skin-popping), intramuscularly (with drugs such as steroids) or intravenously, which is the fastest and most efficient way of getting the drug into the bloodstream. It is almost without exception the riskiest method, too.

The mood and expectations of the user. Some drugs are particularly associated with time and place because the locations influence the perceived effects. Others are dependent upon the mood of the user – particularly drugs with hallucinogenic effects, such as LSD, magic mushrooms, solvents and cannabis. Alcohol's effects too can be greatly influenced by how we feel at the time. If we are happy and relaxed, alcohol is likely to add to this mood, but if we are depressed it can make things seem worse. The importance of our mental state is shown by the placebo effect of many drugs:[2] individuals who are psychologically addicted to a drug feel better just for having the drug in their hand or ready to use. Thus smokers may relax even when they put an unlit cigarette in their mouth, while tranquillizer users often feel better as soon as they have swallowed a tablet, long before it has had chance to have a pharmacological effect.

Classifying drugs

Drugs are often broadly grouped according to the sort of effect they have on our bodies. 'Uppers' or stimulants give more energy and keep us awake. Caffeine, cocaine, amphetamine and Ecstasy are stimulants. 'Downers' or depressants slow our bodies down and make us sleepy. Alcohol, tranquillizers, heroin and painkillers are depressants. Hallucinogens make us see, think and feel things that are not really there. LSD and magic mushrooms are hallucinogens. A few drugs are more complicated and combine some of the effects of the first three groups. For example, solvents affect co-ordination, speech and movement while also giving hallucinations; cannabis relaxes, distorts time, enhances the senses and increases appetite; while tobacco aids concentration yet also relaxes us. The remainder of this chapter will look at most of the substances that are commonly misused, their effects and the context of their use.

Stimulants ('uppers')

Stimulants are drugs that stimulate the central nervous system, increasing alertness, decreasing fatigue and delaying sleep, and heightening mood and concentration.

Cocaine

Cocaine comes from the leaves of the South American coca plant. In its original leaf form Andean Indians have chewed it for thousands of years, obtaining a mild stimulant effect that increases energy and confidence. It provides an often undernourished people with almost all of the daily vitamins they need, and also aids breathing in the extreme altitude. The leaf form contains only about 2% cocaine, whereas cocaine hydrochloride, the form in which it is used in most countries today, contains over 90% cocaine. Cocaine was first extracted around 150 years ago, and in America and Europe was thought efficacious enough to be an active ingredient in chewing gum, cigarettes, coca wines and Coca-Cola – from which it was finally removed in 1904 and replaced by caffeine. Robert Louis Stevenson wrote *Dr Jekyll and Mr Hyde* in six days flat while using cocaine. Queen Victoria and Sigmund Freud were also known users of the drug.

Cocaine is a powerful substance, and though it has developed a glitzy image associated with wealth and fame, as supply has increased so prices have dropped, and in Britain people of all classes and social situations now use it. As a powder it is usually sniffed (known as 'snorting') or injected, but cocaine can also be made into a smokable form known as crack or rock. The effects are very rapid and last for less than an hour, giving intense feelings of strength, confidence and energy. Although cocaine is not physically addictive, its sheer intensity and the feelings of super-confidence make it easy to become mentally dependent. Stopping after regular use can make users feel flat and depressed, while high doses can lead to distorted thinking and paranoia.

It is illegal to possess it, give it to friends or sell it.

Amphetamine

Amphetamine is a laboratory-made substance synthesized over a hundred years ago, but not developed commercially until the 1930s. It was first used in bronchial inhalers, for the treatment of narcolepsy and as a slimming aid, but its real value was found to be as an energy-boosting pep pill. During the Second World War millions of amphetamine tablets were given to British, American and German troops to overcome battle fatigue and boost their confidence. Hitler used large amounts of amphetamine, and at times both Winston Churchill and, later, John F. Kennedy received amphetamine injections. In the 1960s, pharmaceutically manufactured amphetamine pills were widely available, and so-called purple hearts became the darling of many young club-goers in swinging London. In response to the moral panic that this caused, possession of amphetamine was made illegal, and eventually the pharmaceutical supply was brought under control, only to be replaced by the illegally manufactured amphetamine sulphate powder that is now both cheap and commonplace.

Its colour varies between white, pink and yellow, and it is taken by being swallowed, sniffed or injected. Its commonly used names 'speed', 'fast' and 'whizz' give the best clues to its effects, namely lots of energy, alertness and confidence, all useful to late-night club-goers, long-distance lorry-drivers and students, as well as to anyone wanting to lose weight or boost their self-confidence rapidly. The effects last for several hours. After using amphetamine regularly, fatigue and depression set in because the drug has simply used up energy from the body, which needs time to recover. This 'come-down' is hard to handle, and some people take more of the drug at this point to get a further lift, or use depressant drugs to block out the bad feelings.

Too great a use of amphetamine over a period of time

causes loss of weight and can lead to anxious, suspicious thoughts. A few people develop amphetamine psychosis, an acute mental illness marked by paranoia and delusions. Amphetamine is not physically addictive, but it is easy to become mentally dependent upon it and difficult to stop.

It is illegal to possess it, give it to friends or sell it.

Caffeine

Caffeine is the most widely used drug of all and comes in drinks such as coffee, tea, chocolate and Coca-Cola. It is also a constituent of many pain-relief tablets and flu-remedies available from chemists. Caffeine makes us feel more awake, gives us energy and helps concentration: 'I need my cup of coffee in the morning to get going.' Too much caffeine can cause anxiety and irritability, and technically it is possible to overdose on it, though this is extremely rare. Many people are dependent upon caffeine; they are often unaware of this, but if they suddenly stopped drinking tea, coffee or cola drinks they would probably experience withdrawal effects such as headaches and increased tiredness. It can be quite difficult to give it up.

It is legal for anyone of any age to have caffeine and legal to sell it.

Ecstasy

Although it was first discovered in the early years of the twentieth century, Ecstasy became popular in the UK only in the 1980s, when it became associated with the rave scene and dance music. Ecstasy is manufactured in laboratories in the form of pills and capsules that are usually swallowed. It is known by many different names such as 'E', 'doves' and 'rhubarb and custard', according to colour and design. Ecstasy has a stimulant effect, but its hallucinogenic qualities give it a broader feel. The effects include calmness and a sense of pleasure, heightened perception of sounds and feelings and an absence of anger and hostility. For many young people, Ecstasy opened up a new vista where people could have fun and a sense of unity, in marked contrast to the hostility and violence surrounding alcohol. As use has continued, the risks have become more widely known; heatstroke, dehydration or drinking too much water to compensate for the dehydration.[3] Research is now indicating longer-term harm from Ecstasy, including liver damage, potential memory impairment and long-term chemical imbalances in the brain. Deaths associated with Ecstasy have been remarkably few in numbers, albeit widely publicized.

It is illegal to possess it, give it to friends or sell it.

Depressants ('downers')

Depressants are drugs that act on the central nervous system, slowing the body down, relieving tension and anxiety, and aiding sleep. Alcohol, heroin, tranquillizers, painkillers and barbiturates are all depressant drugs. The body becomes tolerant to most depressants, so that more is needed to get the same effect. Taking a lot of any of these drugs will cause drowsiness and sleep, while too much can cause unconsciousness and even death. It is very dangerous to take any of these depressant drugs in combination.

Alcohol

While this drug needs little introduction, it is this very familiarity which has led to widespread disregard for its dangers and consequences. Humans have known how to ferment alcohol for thousands of years, and it has been a central part of the social and religious customs of most societies.

Alcoholic drinks consist of water and ethyl alcohol, produced by fermenting grain, fruits or vegetables. Beer is around one part alcohol to twenty parts water, while wine is about one part alcohol to eight parts water. The process of distillation, producing much stronger 'spirits', has been known for about a thousand years. The main spirits in the UK are whisky, brandy, gin, vodka and rum, which consist of about half alcohol, half water.

reference

Drinking in the UK probably reached its peak in the eighteenth and nineteenth centuries when the grim conditions of the Industrial Revolution made the availability of cheap gin particularly attractive for the toiling masses. Drinking establishments even provided places where the intoxicated could lie down until they were sober again, precursors of today's chill-out areas in clubs. High taxation and reduced access to alcohol through licensing and limited opening hours gradually brought the worst excesses under control, but it took until the First World War for these measures to be fully put in place. In the United States the Prohibition experiment showed that it was impossible to prevent the illicit production and consumption of alcohol, so much so that in some places alcohol consumption actually increased during the Prohibition years. The difficulty in controlling the supply of and demand for alcohol, the involvement of organized crime and the fortunes that were made provide important lessons in our attempt to control other drugs today.

In small amounts alcohol makes us feel relaxed, happy and talkative, hence its importance as a social lubricant. When it is taken in greater amounts, concentration is lost, reactions are poor and clumsy and we lose self-control. Large amounts make a person unconscious. The effects last for several hours, but longer if a lot is consumed. If used to excess, it can cause harm to the brain, liver, heart and stomach. Many people become physically dependent upon alcohol, marked by painful and unpleasant withdrawals when the drug is not taken. Most of these people and many others are also psychologically dependent on drink, relying on it to help them cope with life.

It is illegal to give alcohol to a child under five years of age, legal for anyone over five years old to drink it away from a pub, and legal for persons over eighteen to buy it from licensed premises. It is illegal to sell it without a special licence.

Heroin

Heroin is a painkiller made from morphine, which in turn is made from opium, a natural secretion of the opium poppy. In this form, the drug has been used for thousands of years, medically as a painkiller and socially as a source of great pleasure. Heroin was first discovered in 1874, deriving its name from the German word *heroisch*, meaning 'powerful'. It is eight times stronger than morphine, for which it was first thought to be a non-dependent cure. Morphine and heroin (the latter known in medical contexts as diamorphine) are used in pain control, particularly in cancer sufferers but increasingly in childbirth. Its availability and use as a street drug in the UK have increased since around 1970, so that what used to be available only in large cities can now be obtained by anyone who wants to get some, regardless of where they live. Common names include 'smack', 'brown' and 'skag'. Heroin slows down breathing and other body functions, relaxes muscles and removes physical and mental pain. The big problems in life and the little day-to-day irritations disappear, anxiety and depression giving way to a sense of well-being and detachment. Large amounts cause sleep, unconsciousness and ultimately death.

Heroin can be a white or grey powder, but nowadays it is almost always a brown powder that is smoked or injected, though it can be sniffed. It does not cause much damage to the body by itself; most harm comes from the way it is used (particularly injecting) and from the dependency that can quickly build up, leading to self-neglect, loss of weight, financial difficulties and unpleasant physical withdrawals ('cold turkey') compounded by prolonged mental dependence. Coming off heroin is hard, but staying off it is the real battle. When a drug wraps you in cotton wool and takes away all of life's problems, coping with everyday irritants and setbacks can be too much for individuals trying to stop. Relapse is common, not because of weakness but because it often takes several attempts for people to stay clean.

It is illegal to possess heroin, unless prescribed by a doctor, and illegal to give it away or sell it.

Methadone

Methadone has become well known as a result of its use to minimize the harm experienced by individuals who are dependent on heroin. It is longer-lasting, so does not need to be taken as regularly as heroin; and, since it is most often prescribed as a linctus to be drunk, it does not entail the problems of injecting. The general aim is to give heroin users gradually declining amounts of the drug, thus weaning them off dependence without the usual unpleasant physical effects. The psychological dependence remains, however. Methadone is sometimes provided on a long-term basis known as maintenance prescribing. Methadone is said by many users to be more addictive than heroin, and as it lacks the 'buzz' associated with using, there is a tendency to top up on other substances or to trade it for money or alternatives. The fact that there are now more deaths involving methadone than involving heroin illustrates the problem.

It is illegal to possess methadone unless prescribed by a doctor, and illegal to give it away or sell it.

Other painkillers

Because of the central importance of pain control in many areas of medicine, there is a range of other painkillers that are used and misused, irrespective of whether their source is legitimate through a doctor or illicit on the streets. These include drugs such as Temgesic (buprenorphine), Palfium (dextromoramide), DF118s (dihydrocodeine tartrate), diconal (containing dipipanone hydrochloride), and codeine. People who are prescribed these for pain control can become physically and psychologically dependent upon them and may have difficulties if they try to stop, particularly when taking or exceeding the maximum dose.

These drugs are deemed sufficiently dangerous to make possession illegal unless prescribed by a doctor, and it is illegal to give away or sell them.

Tranquillizers

This is the most widely prescribed class of drug in Britain. Current estimates suggest that 5% of men and 12% of women take them on a daily basis for a month or more during the course of a year.[4] Swallowed as pills or capsules and very occasionally injected, they give feelings of calmness and relaxation, while higher doses induce sleep. Although much safer than their forerunners, barbiturates, tranquillizers are very dangerous when mixed with alcohol or painkillers such as heroin or methadone, and these cocktails are a frequent cause of drug deaths. Most tranquillizers belong to the group of drugs known as the benzodiazepines. This includes Valium (diazepam), temazepam, Mogadon (nitrazepam), Ativan (lorazepam) and Librium (chlordiazepoxide), though there are dozens more.

Like most newly marketed drugs, the benzodiazepines were at first said to be harmless and non-addictive. Time and the pain and distress of thousands of people have given the lie to this. Not only is it very easy to become dependent on tranquillizers, but they induce unpleasant physical and mental withdrawals, as intense and much-longer lasting than most other drugs, including heroin. In consequence, the makers of Valium, the most widely used tranquillizer, now advise that a maximum daily dose of 30mg should be taken for no longer than four weeks.

There is a massive illegal market in all of the benzodiazepines, particularly Valium and temazepam, which are often taken by the handful and, even more dangerously, mixed with alcohol. It is illegal to possess most of these tranquillizers unless they are prescribed, and it is illegal to give them away or sell them.

Hallucinogens

Hallucinogenic drugs distort perception, altering thoughts and distorting the way people see and hear their surroundings. The effects of hallucinogenic drugs are greatly conditioned by the setting and the user's mood. LSD and magic mushrooms are the best-known hallucinogens in the UK. While cannabis, Ecstasy and solvents have hallucinogenic properties, they also have other effects, so they do not fall neatly into the category of hallucinogens.

LSD

LSD was discovered in 1943 by Albert Hoffman, a Swiss chemist engaged on research into the fungus ergot, which grows on rye. It was well known that ergot caused mental disturbances; in the Middle Ages there were cases of entire villages going temporarily mad from ergot poisoning caused by badly stored damp grain or old rye bread.[5] After it was first discovered, LSD was tested by the military on its own soldiers, initially as a weapon and then as a truth drug, but in both circumstances it proved unreliable. Psychiatrists then took it up as a therapeutic tool, but again it was quickly dropped because of the unpredictability of its effects. Finally it leaked on to the open market, and in the 1960s and '70s became widely associated with the hippie movement with its concern for enlightenment and understanding. LSD use slumped in the early 1980s, but it has returned to become one of the most widely used illegal drugs in Britain, more for 'a laugh' than a quest for universal truths.

LSD is the most powerful illicit drug in use, needing as little as a millionth of a gram to have an effect, though most doses are between 25 and 50µg. This is still a tiny amount – a postage stamp is 2,000 times heavier. A dose of 50µg will give a trip that could last for as long as eight to twelve hours. LSD is usually swallowed on squares of paper known as 'trips', or 'tabs'. Names for it are based on the pictures printed on the paper squares, such as 'smilies', 'strawberries', 'penguins' and many hundreds more. LSD makes colours brighter and it changes sounds-perception and thoughts. Over the duration of a trip, mood and experiences change, and what can seem entertaining or awesome can become intensely frightening and disturbing. Despite its strength, LSD is not physically addictive and psychological dependence is very rare. It is fair to say that although there are many stories about alleged LSD-induced accidents, there is little evidence for these. There is some suggestion that LSD can induce psychosis, but it seems that this is mainly a risk for people who are already predisposed to mental health problems.

It is illegal to possess it, give it away or sell it.

Magic mushrooms

Psychoactive plants have been used in many societies and cultures for hundreds of years. In America the peyote cactus was used by native Americans, while mushrooms were eaten in Siberia and Lapland. In Britain there are two types of magic mushroom, liberty caps and fly agaric. These grow wild and have effects similar to, but slightly milder than, LSD. They are usually eaten or drunk as a tea, and the effects can last up to eight hours. Because only two of the 230 types of British mushroom are psychoactive, one of the biggest dangers to would-be users lies in collecting the wrong sort, especially some of the poisonous ones. The psychoactive drug in magic mushrooms is psilocybin.

It is not an offence to pick magic mushrooms, but as soon as there is an attempt to extract the drug by drying, boiling or cooking them they become illegal to possess, sell or give away.

Other drugs

Finally, there are those drugs which do not fit neatly into any group, because they combine the effects of some of the earlier categories.

Cannabis (marijuana)

This is the most widely used illegal drug in Britain. The plant grows wild in many places in the world. The fibrous stems have been used through the ages for making hemp rope and paper, and the leaves and seeds for a variety of herbal remedies and intoxicating substances. In Britain the

reference

celebrated seventeenth-century herbalist Culpeper listed a number of medical uses for cannabis. Queen Victoria was treated with tincture of cannabis by her doctor, who described the drug as 'one of the most therapeutic agents we possess'.[6] At that time, cannabis was never widely used in Britain as an intoxicant, but in the West Indian colonies it was popular among the slaves, becoming an important part of the growing Rastafarian movement in the postwar years. In America it was closely associated with the jazz and blues musicians of the 1930s, but its use really took off there only in the 1960s, when it became an integral part of the West Coast movement. As a result its popularity grew in Europe and the UK. Even so, it is only since the late 1980s that its use has spread beyond students, the middle classes and Rastafarians to reach the whole of British society. People of all classes and ages now use it. Interestingly, the claims for the medical efficacy of cannabis are once again being heard, particularly for people with multiple sclerosis and glaucoma and those experiencing nausea as a result of cancer treatments. As one of the first popular illegal drugs, it always received a negative press with quite ludicrous stories,[7] and it is still a subject which raises the fiercest debates and gives rise to some of the most value-laden drug research.

Cannabis is used in its natural form, the dried leaves being smoked with or without tobacco. This form is most commonly known as 'draw', 'blow', 'grass', 'bush' or 'weed'. The resin is obtained from the tops of the female flowers and can be smoked or eaten. This has numerous national and regional names, such as 'hash', 'dope', 'puff' and 'tac'. Cannabis oil is a very concentrated form of the drug, but is rarely available in the UK. There are probably hundreds of different types and forms of cannabis, and the growth in the world market has seen new forms of cannabis, such as 'skunk' and 'Northern Lights', cultivated to increase the potency of the main psychoactive ingredient THC.[8]

The effects of cannabis vary, depending upon mood, how strong the brand is and how much is taken, but it usually makes users feel relaxed, talkative and giggly. Time and perception are distorted, and, while sounds, colours and thoughts are often enhanced, cannabis can cause feelings of anxiety and disturbance, particularly among inexperienced or heavy users. Cannabis certainly affects co-ordination and concentration, and can affect short-term memory. It increases feelings of hunger, often referred to as 'the munchies'. The effects of cannabis start quickly and can last for a few hours. Even when used regularly it does not cause physical dependence, but stopping can be mentally hard for many people who come to depend upon it to relax or help them to sleep. The other main problem resulting from cannabis is drug-induced lethargy, particularly in young users who smoke it morning, noon and night and cannot be bothered to do anything else. Most of the accounts of physical harm from cannabis are hotly contested, but there is undoubtedly evidence that smoking it heavily affects the lungs and is potentially carcinogenic.

It is illegal to possess it, grow it, give it away or sell it.

Solvents

Aerosols, glue, petrol, cigarette lighter fuel and other volatile substances give off fumes that are inhaled to get high. The effects last a short time and cause hallucinations, dizziness, loss of self-control and co-ordination, and impaired balance that looks like drunkenness. Most risk comes from choking and suffocation, but aerosols are particularly dangerous, causing freezing of the larynx. It is estimated that a third of deaths resulting from aerosol use occurs in first-time users. Solvents are not physically addictive, but there is clear evidence of strong psychological dependence, making it a very hard habit to give up. It is widespread throughout the world, wherever volatile chemicals are available. In the UK it often starts among the nine to fourteen age group, and use is usually relatively short-term, giving way to the use of other substances, such as cannabis and alcohol, that are deemed more grown-up. Those who continue to use solvents run the risk of physical problems such as kidney, liver, brain and heart damage. Surprisingly, over half of all deaths from volatile substances occur in those over eighteen years of age.[9]

reference

It is not illegal to possess solvents, but it is illegal for shopkeepers to sell them to young people under the age of eighteen if they suspect they are misusing them.

Nicotine

Nicotine and tobacco are so commonplace that their methods of use need little introduction. This has not always been so. As with other drugs, acceptability is dependent on culture and other values. In the Ottoman Empire, nicotine users were beheaded or hung, drawn and quartered, while in Russia they were tortured to give details of their supplier. King James I described tobacco as a 'loathsome and stinking weed' and imposed a 4,000% tax increase that makes present-day Chancellors of the Exchequer look decidedly soft. In Britain, taking snuff was a fashionable habit towards the end of the seventeenth century and throughout the eighteenth, but, as this habit spread down to the poorer folk, the gentry took up cigar-smoking instead. Cigarettes became popular with the troops returning from the Crimean War towards the middle of the nineteenth century, and the extent of cigarette use increased steadily, with the beginning of what have now become the multi-national tobacco companies. Smoking reached a peak in the middle of the twentieth century, when over half the adult population smoked, but it has steadily declined in popularity since then.

Nicotine is obtained from the tobacco plant, whose dried leaves are smoked or chewed. Nicotine has the effect of relaxing the user and increasing concentration and alertness. It is easy to become dependent, and most smokers feel irritable and depressed if they try to stop. The biggest risk comes from the way the drug is used. Cigarette smoke contains over 3,000 chemicals, and smoking causes many health problems for users – particularly heart and lung damage and a high level of cancer.

It is legal to possess or use tobacco products, but illegal to sell them to someone known to be under sixteen.

A growing list

This is by no means a complete list of the drugs that are used and misused.[10] Other substances, such as steroids, barbiturates, ketamine, nitrites and Prozac, are also commonplace. As new substances are discovered in legal and illegal laboratories or by those exploring the natural world, the list of drugs that are used and misused will undoubtedly continue to grow.

reference

chapter **four**

the reasons

> Alice ventured to taste it, and finding it very nice,
> (it had, in fact, a sort of mixed flavour of cherry-
> tart, custard, pineapple, roast turkey, toffee
> and hot buttered toast,) she very soon finished
> it off.

Why do people take drugs? There is (of course) no simple answer. We are complex beings and our reasons are complicated and varied. And the reason we continue to use a drug may be different from the reason we started.

Nevertheless, there are some common features and patterns that we can trace. These can be seen in the use of alcohol as well as of illegal drugs.

As we saw earlier, people first use drugs in an experimental way. A mixture of curiosity and risk-taking generally fuels this experimentation, but peer involvement or the desire for a particular image and status may reinforce it. Precisely which drug people try at this stage depends upon how much money they have to spend, their access to and the availability of particular substances, and the sort of people they mix with. A well-paid business executive is more likely to try premium lagers or dabble in cocaine, whereas an unemployed person with little money to spare is more likely to use solvents, drink cheap cider or get hold of some Valium.[1] The drugs most commonly used by young people, such as alcohol, cannabis,

LSD, poppers and amphetamine, are at the cheaper end of the market and quite widely available.

Once people have experimented with a drug or a number of drugs, they may decide to stop because they did not value the experience, they feared the risk, or they have satisfied the 'I'll try anything once' approach to life. If they continue to take the substance(s), however, it will no longer be out of a sense of curiosity, but because they like the effect or feel that they gain something from taking it. For them it is a desirable, positive experience that they wish to repeat. The following are the commonest reasons for wanting to do so.

Enjoyment and pleasure

If sex is the most fun you can have without laughing, as Woody Allen once said, drugs can't be far behind. Most people get into drugs because they enjoy the experience and it makes them feel good. This is probably the single most important reason for using drugs. It is surprising how often this has been overlooked, denied or conveniently ignored. Some of the early drug education programmes that focused on the negative consequences of drugs, using shock and fear as deterrents, appear to have had little impact on subsequent drug use because they distorted the true picture.[2] When the film *Trainspotting* was first released, it was criticized for showing drug-taking as an enjoyable experience. Yet to ignore this fundamental reason for drug use not only presents a dishonest account but hinders our understanding of the reasons behind the behaviour.

In the Carnegie Medal-winning novel *Junk*, one of the central characters explains the enjoyment: 'Look, drugs are fun. They make you feel good, that's all. Sure they're powerful, that's why they're dangerous. So is life.'[3] Excitement and danger are part of the fun, and, in young people's eyes, getting a buzz is a crucial factor in defining the worth of an activity. Drugs provide many of them with this buzz, because they give instant feelings of excitement, euphoria, confidence and release. Not that this is anything new. The pursuit of pleasure and happiness has always been a major driving force behind the use of drugs and alcohol. Writing in 1822, Thomas De Quincy was enthusiastic about his first experience of opium: 'Here was a panacea, a cure for all human woes; here was the secret of happiness about which philosophers had disputed for so many ages; happiness might now be bought for a penny and carried in the waistcoat pocket.'[4] In our own day, one of the main reasons for the growing popularity of crack cocaine lies in the massive 'rush' of pleasure which is experienced a mere seven seconds after smoking the drug.[5]

The enjoyment factor also depends on where the drug is used and the mood of the user. In the wrong frame of mind, the wrong company or the wrong place, drugs can be far from fun. This is especially true of hallucinogenic substances such as LSD, magic mushrooms or Ecstasy, but even with a less intense drug such as alcohol, context and mood are important influences on its effects. Someone who is alone and depressed is unlikely to feel happy as a result of drinking half a bottle of whisky (though it may help him to forget why he is depressed). By contrast, drinking a small amount of alcohol with friends at a lively bar may well be a pleasant experience. Because of the influence of these external factors, first-time users of LSD and Ecstasy are often advised to take the drug in the company of a more experienced friend or acquaintance who will guide them through any bad effects.

One person recalls her first use of Ecstasy: 'I was intrigued by its name. My curiosity was heightened after talking to a knowledgeable enthusiast called Rick ... He reassured me that he would be there for me. He then gave me a paper outlining the basis on which the session was to be run, with regard to safety and propriety, giving me the option of his remaining a minder or joining me on the trip. I opted for the former and then got on with it.'[6]

The experience of cannabis (marijuana) may also need to be guided, or at least put into context.

Marijuana-produced sensations are not automatically or necessarily pleasurable. The taste for such an experience is a socially acquired one, not different in kind from an acquired taste for oysters or dry Martinis. The user feels dizzy, thirsty; his scalp tingles, he misjudges time and distances. Are these things pleasurable? He isn't sure. If he is to continue marijuana use, he must decide that they are.[7]

Users of alcohol, tobacco or heroin also need to learn to enjoy the effects, which may not be immediately apparent, since first-time use of these drugs often causes nausea and sickness. Here too it is possible to learn quickly how to appreciate the pleasurable feelings and to control, avoid or minimize the negative experiences. 'I like being sick on any drug ... The very first time I had a full Ecstasy pill to myself was the very first night I went out clubbing. I remember I threw up and after I threw up I felt amazing. I felt brilliant. I must have introduced myself to everyone in the club that night.'[7] The unpleasantness of an alcohol hangover does little to deter people from drinking. Few individuals would continue to use any of these substances if they were not pleasurable. Irrespective of our own experiences or opinions, enjoyment is probably the single most important reason people use drugs and alcohol.

Cultural reasons

Cultural acceptability of a substance is an important factor in determining whether people use it. As we have already seen, acceptability within a culture changes over time, and there is also considerable variation between countries and cultures as to which drugs are acceptable and which are not. In the UK, many people start to drink because it is culturally acceptable – indeed, in some places it is almost a cultural requirement. Because I grew up in the heavy-drinking culture of northeast England, drinking large quantities of alcohol and being good at it appeared to me to be necessary not just to become one of the lads but simply to blend in with the social and cultural background. More widely, alcohol is regarded as an essential part of weddings and parties, Christmas and New Year celebrations, holidays and sporting events – witness the

Hogmanay festivities on television or the teatime crowd at a Test match.

Subcultural groups also have a bearing on drug use, particularly on substances that are illegal or socially unacceptable. For example, Rastafarians may accept cannabis use, Ecstasy may be acceptable within the club culture and the use of steroids may be tolerated by some groups of bodybuilders, but within society as a whole these substances are generally not acceptable. Some subcultures develop around drug use and become specifically drug subcultures, people being members by virtue of their drug use. Many of those with long-term drug and alcohol problems find that their only acquaintances are within these subcultures.

However strongly the use of a drug is tolerated within a culture or subculture, there are always other reasons a person chooses to use it, and cultural influences alone cannot explain drug use.

Peer influence

In the case of young people, in particular, the influence of peers is popularly seen as significant in determining drug use. The term 'peer pressure' has now come into common parlance. The need for approval and acceptance is so powerful that individuals, particularly young people, will conform to the activities of their peers to avoid rejection. It is an appealing notion, not least because it is easy to empathize with the need to belong and to conform. Many adults can recall the importance of these in their own teenage years, and may indeed find that such needs still influence their behaviour. In the case of young people, it is important to remember that whatever pressure there may be to use drugs, there is also peer pressure not to use drugs. Not all young people see drugs as a positive and exciting option. 'I think they're stupid because when they take it they show themselves up. They think they're dead hard or something … by taking the drug.'[9]

Despite the appeal of peer pressure as an explanation why people use drugs, research suggests that it is a little more complicated than this. Peer pressure plays a part, especially if the choice of people to mix with is limited, but often it is peer preference that influences decisions. We choose to be members of particular groups with their influences and interests, whether sport or a hobby, or an intellectual, political or religious activity. Similarly, young people select friendship networks on the basis of music, fashion, sport and other interests, including drug use. Some may stick with peer groups using no substances, others with those who smoke cigarettes (we may recall the smokers at school hanging around together), others with those who use alcohol and some with those who use a variety of substances. This pattern of peer preferences and activities is still with us in adult life and continues to determine our behaviour.

Specific effects

One of the main reasons people carry on using drugs after experimentation is to continue to experience specific effects that they like or desire. These fall into five categories.

Physical reasons

Drugs provide various desirable physical effects.

Energy and staying power are particularly associated with stimulant drugs: a strong cup of tea or coffee to start the day, or amphetamine taken by students, long-distance lorry-drivers, club-goers and soldiers in order to stay awake through the night.

Weight loss was one of the main purposes of prescription amphetamines during the 1960s, and many people, particularly young women, use amphetamine to control their weight (or at least, see this as a valuable adjunct to its other desirable effects). Most of the high-street slimming clinics offering wonder treatments for weight loss are simply prescribing a form of amphetamine.

Enhancement of sexual experiences is attributed to many drugs, particularly stimulants. There seems to be some truth in the link between cocaine and sex, not just in terms of enhancing sex but as a similarly euphoric experience. As one young woman said after first trying crack, 'It's like the best sex you could ever have.' Research and anecdotal evidence indicate that some of the reports surrounding amphetamine and Ecstasy are exaggerated. While these drugs may increase desire and feelings of sexual awareness, they can also impair performance.[10]

Drugs such as alcohol, cannabis and opium have been used to induce *sleep* for thousands of years. Over recent decades, barbiturates and tranquillizers have become popular aids to sleep, and an increasing number of people use cannabis as a late-night relaxant and sleeping agent.

Improved performance, increased body size and speed of recovery from exertion are particularly associated with drugs such as anabolic steroids. For many body-builders or club doormen who want to get big (or even bigger), this is an attractive proposition.

Psychological and emotional reasons

To help us be sociable, bright and witty is an important reason for the use of many drugs, none more so than alcohol. A party without alcohol would be seen by many people as lacking the vital ingredient to make it go well. Interestingly, for all alcohol's supposed virtues as a social lubricant, the fine line between alcohol-induced harmony and aggression led to one of the great attractions of Ecstasy. Many Ecstasy users talked disparagingly of so-called 'beer-monsters'. For women in particular, there was great pleasure in feeling in control of their destiny. Instead of having drunks slobbering over them in night-clubs, they found that men on E could be open and warm rather than macho.[11] Cannabis too is seen as being a positive social mixer.

Building up confidence is another important reason people use drugs. Some drugs, particularly depressants, may block out inhibitions – the so-called 'Dutch courage' provided by alcohol or the reduction in anxiety caused by Valium. Other drugs, particularly stimulants such as cocaine and amphetamine, provide a massive boost in confidence; if they don't actually put you on top of the world, you feel as if you are ready to conquer it. This can seem desirable to any of us, but it is especially attractive to those with low levels of confidence and self-esteem. Such people are particularly vulnerable to developing a psychological dependence on these substances, as are those who use drugs to overcome anxiety and fear. 'Heroin is the best drug on the planet for taking away hang-ups,' writes C. J. Stone. 'You become Mr Intelligent, Mr Confident ... Things are so apparently uncomplicated in that state that you begin to yearn for it all the time ... Maybe I'm never honest, never straightforward, never intelligent, never confident without it.'[12]

Many people also use drugs as a *means of escape*. It may be only an occasional release, a drowning of sorrows now and then, but this can easily become a regular pattern of dealing with bad feelings or memories, unhappiness and loneliness. To some extent any drug used regularly will provide this escape, but the different types of drugs have different escape destinations. Stimulants take us away to a brighter, exciting world, hallucinogens to a weird, wonderful and unpredictable world, while depressants such as heroin, alcohol or Valium will 'switch out the lights' and provide the ultimate escape of oblivion. Painkilling drugs such as heroin, morphine, Temgesic and DF118s are particularly attractive because they kill both emotional and physical pain. As one person put it, 'Heroin is like being wrapped in a nice warm blanket.' Many people who have been prescribed painkillers by their GP for genuine physical reasons continue to take the medication long after they should do so, because of the drug's capacity to ease some of the emotional and psychological inconveniences in life.

Spiritual reasons

While some of the reasons we have discussed undoubtedly have spiritual connections, there are also distinct spiritual reasons for drug use. Drugs are seen as offering a mind-expanding experience and have been used for this purpose for many centuries. In some cases they even take

on a sacramental significance, as cannabis does for Rastafarians, the peyote cactus for native Americans and sacred
mushrooms for the Aztecs. The use of drugs to expand
consciousness reached a new height in the 1960s with the
growth of the counter-culture and the influence of Timothy
Leary, self-appointed prophet and high priest of LSD, who
advocated the drug as a means of deep meditation. The area
of spirituality and drugs is explored more fully in chapter 9.

Creativity

Drugs have long been used to stimulate ideas and gain new
perspectives in most of the creative arts. The use of opiates by
poets such as Byron, Keats, Coleridge, Shelley and Elizabeth
Barrett Browning is well documented. Robert Louis Stevenson used cocaine, Sir Walter Scott took large quantities of
laudanum and opium, while Aldous Huxley experimented
with both mescaline and LSD. Dylan Thomas and Anthony
Burgess are two of many authors who have written books
while under the influence of alcohol. Sherlock Holmes, the
fictional detective, was a user of cocaine. He explains its
attraction to the disapproving Dr Watson: 'I suppose that its
influence is physically a bad one. I find it, however, so
transcendently stimulating and clarifying to the mind that its
secondary action is a matter of small moment.'[13]

The disinhibiting effects of many drugs are associated
with dance in numerous societies. Popular dance in the UK
has recently been profoundly influenced by Ecstasy. Visual
art too has been influenced by the use of substances. Like the
poets with their opiates, the tortured minds of many painters
have been eased by alcohol; absinthe was favoured by
numerous French and Dutch painters in the nineteenth
century. Pop musicians have also been associated with drugs
and alcohol – never more so than since the 1960s, when
songs influenced by drugs or with overt references to drugs
(both for and against) have abounded. Within the music
industry, the list of drug and alcohol casualties constantly
grows.

While the quest for creativity and a desire to view the

world from a different perspective certainly encourage musicians, writers and artists to take drugs, it is also true that they often take them for the same reasons as other users.

Dependence

For a small but significant minority of individuals who use substances, an additional reason for continuing to use a particular drug or drugs is physical and psychological dependence. Stopping their particular drug brings physical or mental discomfort, so they continue to use it to avoid these unpleasant feelings. Only some drugs will cause physical withdrawal symptoms such as shivering, shaking, sleeplessness and anxiety, but, for people who are physically addicted, avoidance of these symptoms is a crucial reason for continuing to take the drug, however self-destructive this may appear to others. In the words of William Burroughs, 'Junk takes everything and gives nothing but an insurance against junk sickness.'[14]

In contrast, all drugs can lead to mental and psychological dependence. This is a major reason for continuing to use substances and is in the long run far harder to overcome than physical dependence. For many, even the rituals of use are a part of the dependency, whether this is lifting a cigarette to the mouth, inserting a needle in the vein or holding a glass in the hand. With dependence, the excitement of looking cool and getting high in the early stages of drug use has long since evaporated, leaving behind the monotony and grind of obtaining and using the drug just to feel normal. Nobody ever thinks it will happen to them, but for a significant minority of drug users, dependence and addiction become the single most important reason for continuing their habit.

Why do people use drugs? Yes, they help us relax and forget a bad day at work. Yes, they help us appear bright and witty in company, and sometimes help us to be creative. But for us to risk the consequences that we do (our health, our relationships, our liberty), there must be some deeper underlying reasons as well.

part **two**

drugs <u>and</u> christianity

in the beginning

> 'One side will make you grow taller, and the
> other side will make you grow shorter.'
>   'One side of what? The other side of what?'
> thought Alice to herself.
>   'Of the mushroom,' said the Caterpillar, just as
> if she had asked it aloud; and in another minute
> it was out of sight.

Nature is full of plants and substances that can be used to change the way we think, feel and behave. If a drug comes from a natural source, does this mean that it is automatically OK to use it? Why do harmful drugs exist if the world that God created was perfect?

Nature's bounty

It is an increasingly popular belief that everything natural is good. Herbalism, homeopathy, naturopathy and aromatherapy, which involve natural treatments, have become so widespread and established that they are now referred to as complementary rather than as alternative forms of medicine. Even listening to natural sounds such as mountain streams or waves on the seashore is thought to be relaxing and harmonizing. Though these ideas do not necessarily conflict with a Christian view of the created order, the vast majority of books on natural healing and the many centres for wholeness have close links with New Age, pagan or deep ecology movements. As a result, the underpinning philosophy of what might be termed the 'natural is good' movement is often sharply at odds with Christianity. Science and technology are believed to have ignored or led us away from ancient truths and wisdom about our relationship with the earth, knowledge that we need to rediscover in order to find our true selves. In its most popular form, people believe that natural things are good simply because they are natural, a view that probably has more to do with advertisement copy-writing than with New Age philosophy.

Just like yam and cabbage

'Cannabis is a beautiful gift from Mother Nature.'[1] It is clearly only a small step to take the idea that 'natural is good' into the realm of mood-altering substances. The reasoning goes something like this. Drugs made or extracted in laboratories using chemicals are dangerous and unpredictable in their effects and likely to cause problems. They are a human product rather than a natural one and should therefore be treated with caution. In contrast, any substance that comes from raw plant material not only carries significantly less risk but is actually beneficial to our health and state of mind. In short, natural drugs are life-enhancing. Thus a man charged with cultivating magic mushrooms declared in his defence that he was 'growing a health food to make the world a better place'.[2] Bob Marley, one of the most famous proponents of cannabis, said, 'Is only a natural t'ing. Herb is the healin' of the nation. Herb just grow like yam and cabbage.'[3]

Recent years have seen a proliferation of natural herbal highs that are available. Most of them are legal, which for many people is an added bonus. Advertisements for these substances are now commonplace in a number of magazines and newspapers. 'Light up, enjoy the taste, feel the instant high. Enter into a new dimension of contentment and satisfaction,' declares one such advert for a combination of stimulant and sedative herbs that can be smoked.[4] A search on the internet reveals over forty-five sites selling legal 'herbal highs', though most carry disclaimers for any adverse effects that might be experienced.[5] Recently 'herbal crack' has been sold as 'the newest of the new in the world of personal chemical enhancement. Best of all, it's natural and legal.'[6] The hype accompanying so-called herbal Ecstasy urges users to 'enjoy natural euphoric sensations from a herbal dietary supplement'.[7] Twenty-five years down the line, the advertising slogan for Consulate cigarettes that were said to be 'as cool as a mountain stream' seems remarkably up to date.

Special effects?

When we look at the character and effects of 'natural' drugs, the argument is rather more complicated than a simple 'natural = good, synthetic = bad' division. Strength or potency is an important factor; the more potent one form of the substance is over another, the more addictive and problematic it is likely to become. In general, natural forms of a drug tend to be less potent and thus less harmful than the refined or synthetic forms. But the difference is relative rather than absolute, and all drugs can cause some degree of harm. For example, coca leaves contain less than 2% cocaine, but when the drug is refined in laboratories it is usually in the region of 85% – 95% pure. The South American Indians who chew the coca leaves often have a mild psychological dependence on the drug, rather similar to the caffeine dependence of tea or coffee drinkers, whereas regular users of the refined cocaine powder can experience severe personal and psychological problems. LSD which is synthetically produced in a laboratory is exceptionally strong compared with its natural equivalent, which occurs in the fungus ergot that grows on rye and other grasses. In spite of this, in the Middle Ages, eating rye bread containing ergot led to disturbing outbreaks of the affliction known as St Anthony's fire, characterized by wild, LSD-like hallucinations. Other plants used for their mind-altering effects include certain mushrooms, nutmeg, some cactuses, morning-glory seeds and so on. Many of these have to be taken in exactly the right amount to get the desired effect and to avoid poisoning. This was certainly true of hemlock, mandrake, belladonna and aconite, highly poisonous plants that were used in precise quantities by medieval witches for their psychedelic effects.[8] While morphine and heroin are significantly more potent than the natural opium from which they are refined,[9] opium can still cause both physical and psychological dependence. Concern about the problem of opium addiction in China was a major factor that led to the nineteenth-century Opium War.[10] Even cannabis, that 'beautiful gift from Mother Nature', can lead to psychological dependence when it is used regularly. With heavy use there is a tendency towards lethargy and withdrawal. The current development of much stronger strains of cannabis such as skunk and Northern Lights will almost certainly increase these associated problems.

All drugs, whether natural or synthetic, have the potential for some level of physical harm and/or psychological dependence. At the same time, it is true that many plants and herbs do have beneficial effects and healing properties and have been used in this capacity for centuries. The problem seems to lie within ourselves rather than with the substance. Human beings seem to find it extremely difficult to use drugs in a wise, temperate manner. Every one of us is liable to misuse drugs, irrespective of whether these are natural or synthetic in origin.

In the beginning

'In the beginning God made dope,' said the teeshirt slogan, bringing us back to our original question about the source of natural drugs. How does their existence fit in with a Christian understanding of creation, in which God made the heavens and the earth and all that is in them?

In the Genesis account, at the end of each day's creative action, it is said that God saw that what he had made was good. When he had finished the whole creation and filled the earth with all sorts of creatures, including humans, 'God saw all that he had made, and it was very good' (Genesis 1:31). The Bible's subsequent account of the fall is extremely clear about its consequences for our relationship with God and the effect of this on all of creation. We are members of a spoiled species. Every part of each of us and all of life as we know it is affected by sin. Our relationship with God, with one another, with our minds, emotions and bodies and with our environment is damaged and lessened by sin. Sin brought death, disruption, distortion and decay in all of the created order, and banishment from the perfection of the Garden of Eden. Plants and vegetation did not escape the consequences. 'Cursed is the ground because of you,' God said to Adam and Eve (Genesis 3:17). St Paul says that 'the whole creation has been groaning' while awaiting liberation from its bondage to decay (Romans 8:22). Sin and its consequences are all around us.

Chance or design?

This leaves four possible explanations for the origin of natural drugs in plants:

- their existence is merely fortuitous;
- plants containing drugs appeared as a twisted consequence of the fall, along with disease, decay and death;
- God gave us plants containing drugs after the fall, as a palliative to help us deal with the pain, separation and death that had become part of our existence; or
- God made all plants, including those containing drugs, during the initial creation.

It is hard to believe that natural drugs appeared completely by chance. There are hundreds of plants which have not only specific physical and psychological effects on the human body but also beneficial or healing properties. For instance, willow bark chewed for centuries as a painkiller was found to contain aspirin. Another bark, taken from the cinchona tree, contains quinine, a substance effective in containing malaria. The small amounts of cocaine in coca leaves not only contain important minerals and trace elements absent elsewhere in the diet of South American Indians, but aid breathing in the rarefied atmosphere of the Andes. The naturally occurring morphine and codeine have proved to be invaluable in providing pain relief, and there is increasing evidence that cannabis reduces some of the problems of glaucoma. The medicinal value of alcohol is mentioned in the Bible. Can these be mere coincidences, or even mutations as a result of the fall? Either solution requires considerable faith. In the biblical picture of God's creation, we see order, complexity and purpose. These were established at creation, and, throughout the Bible, the message that God is the God of order is clear and consistent. This not only seems to negate the idea that psycho-active plants grew by chance or as a twisted consequence of the fall, but also affirms their existence as part of God's creation. So did God create them in the beginning, before the fall?

The Bible creation story implies a natural end to God's work of creating after the sixth day (whether you take that as a literal six days or not). There is no indication that God subsequently added to the creation. Furthermore, to suggest that God gave us psychoactive plants after the fall in order to help us cope with its consequent pain, separation and death sounds rather like Q providing James Bond with a host of technical gadgets and aids to help him through a dangerous mission. If drugs were created as part of God's loving care for us, it makes more sense for this provision to have taken place at the creation and not after the fall. As C. S. Lewis says, it is 'a ridiculous idea that the Fall took God by surprise and upset his plan, or else – more ridiculous still – that God planned the whole thing for conditions which he knew were never going to be realised'.[11] It would seem reasonable to conclude, therefore, that God made psychoactive plants as part of his creation along with 'every seed-bearing plant on the face of the whole earth', 'trees that were pleasing to the eye and good for food' and all his other handiwork that he declared to be 'good' (Genesis 1:29; 2:9; 1:11–12). In the words of the Lutheran Church of Australia, 'Drugs are a good gift to man from God, the Creator.'[12]

A good gift

This is a major difference between the Christian perspective and the 'natural is good' position outlined earlier: that there is God, and he created the world. Our praise and thanksgiving can therefore include our gratitude for the provision of all the natural painkillers, stimulants and sedatives within God's creation and, indeed, those he has enabled us to develop. As the Australian Lutheran Church has affirmed, 'when used responsibly, drugs can be a valuable aid to bodily and mental health and with thanks to God'.[13] Creation and nature 'are signs: their value, their meaning, lies in the fact that they speak to us of God and lead us to him'.[14] It is clear, however, that we should worship God, not his creation, though we can and should celebrate and rejoice at nature's beauty, complexity and variety. When the earth and nature are venerated and worshipped instead of their Creator, or when drugs are elevated to a central, even sacred, place in our lives, we are guilty of idolatry. 'We have lost our way in the enchanted wood, and in seeking for what we have lost we become fixated on the creation rather than using it as a means of communication with the creator.'[15]

The aching void

Idolatry is sin, and the existence of sin is another point of departure from the 'natural is good' position. Of course there are other forms of sin, and, as we have seen, sin has had far-reaching consequences on our lives and relationships. Not only has the alienation caused by sin left us with an aching void that we want to fill, but because our relationship with God and his creation is so distorted we are unable to use his gifts wisely and properly as they were intended. Our relationships, sex, work and eating habits are tainted and distorted, used as analgesics to deaden our pain or meet undefined needs. Likewise our use of drugs. Sin has not only resulted in the alienation that makes drugs desirable; it has also compromised our ability to use them properly. The words of the musician Alice Cooper ring starkly true: 'When you narrow it all down, I think the problem is that we've put ourselves on the throne. We've made man into God and because we're such slaves to our lusts we do a really poor job of being God. We'll give up everything for that girl, that drug, that money; and as far as I see it we need to take ourselves off the throne and put God back on it.'[16]

God at the centre

In the light of all this, we need to be careful about our use of all substances, irrespective of their source. In the same way that a boxer with a tendency to cut easily has to concentrate on protecting himself, we need to take precautions if we wish to safeguard our spiritual health and well-being, ensuring that we put God on the throne where he belongs.

chapter

six

specific bible principles:
alcohol

'If there's no meaning in it,' said the King, 'that
saves a world of trouble, you know, as we
needn't try to find any. And yet I don't know,' he
went on, spreading out the verses on his knee,
and looking at them with one eye; 'I seem to
see some meaning in them after all.'

Is it possible to develop a specifically Christian approach to
the use of drugs? Must we 'just say no', can we ever say yes,
or do we end up settling for definitely maybe? How do we
differentiate between all the substances?

Alcohol is the only currently used drug that is specifically commented upon in the Bible. We do know,
however, that other substances were in use in the area and
during the time span in which the Bible was written.
Potions and the medicinal use of plants were widespread
throughout the Middle East: the Bible mentions a number of plants known to have psychoactive properties, which
grew naturally in Palestine and the surrounding area.
These include wormwood, mandrake, myrrh and gall. Some
present-day drugs were also known. Cannabis and opium
were used in some areas of the Roman Empire, and
scientists have recently found traces of nicotine, cannabis,

opium and cocaine in samples of hair taken from Egyptian mummies.[1]

Alcohol in Bible times[2]

The Bible contains more than 250 references to alcoholic drinks. Essentially these were fermented beer and wine, but many different words are used in the original Hebrew and Greek texts, indicating slight differences between them.[3] New wine, sweet wine, old wine, mixed wine, sour wine, grape juice, beer, strong drink and sweet drink are the main terms used. Distillation was not known at that time, and the quality of yeast, sweeteners and brewing techniques were far inferior to what is now available, meaning that the alcohol levels of these drinks was much lower than in alcoholic beverages produced today. The place of wine and beer in society was also very different. It was conventional for these to be drunk in place of water, which was invariably contaminated and unsafe to drink.[4]

Wine was the popular drink in Israel, where vines grew easily on the hillsides. When the grapes were picked, they were squeezed and sometimes drunk as fresh grape juice, but in general the juice was fermented because this ensured it would keep. The presence of yeasts and sugars in the grape juice, together with the warm climate, made fermentation a natural process – indeed, one that could scarcely be avoided. This natural process of fermentation was, however, harnessed and controlled; in Israel the production of wine was one of the country's principal activities. The first wine of the year came from the juice extracted by treading the grapes in the press. This was usually regarded as the best and strongest. A second batch was made from the residue by squeezing it in the winepress. By New Testament times, the Roman Empire had improved trade routes between countries, and wealthy individuals kept cellars of fine wines from all over the Mediterranean. In Egypt and Babylon, beer was a more common form of alcoholic drink and would probably have been drunk by the Israelites when they were in exile in these countries. Beer was generally made from grain, but in

Babylon it was also made from fruit such as dates. There is a description of a brewery on an Egyptian papyrus document dating from as early as 3500 BC.

The Old Testament and alcohol

The majority of Bible references to wine and beer are in the Old Testament, and there are a number of consistent themes.

There are of course *warnings* about the risks of excessive drinking, the most graphic being in Proverbs and Isaiah.[5] There are also references to wine as a *sign of God's blessing or wrath*. Blessing is often linked to prophetic accounts of the future Israel and promises of abundance, where the mountains and the land drip with wine (*e.g.* Joel 3:18). Conversely, God's judgment is associated with the failure of the vineyards and the absence of wine (*e.g.* Joel 1:10). Other imagery regarding God's judgment alludes to the trampling of the winepress and the wine cup of God's wrath.

Finally, alcohol is frequently mentioned as a *detail of everyday life*, without comment on whether it is good or bad. References to the grape harvest, the production and sale of wine or occupations linked to it, and its use as an offering, as a gift or at meals, banquets and celebrations are commonplace.

The New Testament and alcohol

Wine is mentioned only forty times in the New Testament. The word is almost always *oinos*, referring to grape juice or wine. *Gleukos* refers to new or sweet wine (mentioned on just one occasion: in Peter's Pentecost sermon, when he rebuts accusations that the apostles have had too much wine). The only other New Testament word for wine is *oxos*, or wine vinegar, the cheapest and coarsest of wines. This is mentioned once in each of the Gospels, all recounting the same story of the offer of wine vinegar to Jesus at his crucifixion.

Some of these references are where wine is used as an image, as in the Old Testament. Jesus spoke of old and new wineskins as a parable to illustrate the newness of his message. In the book of Revelation, wine is used to symbolize judgment and wrath.[6] Perhaps the supreme example of imagery remains with us today in the use of wine within the Holy Communion service.

Positive uses of alcohol

Though it sits uncomfortably with those who are strongly opposed to alcohol, it is impossible to ignore Bible references to its positive uses. The following are some of these uses.

To refresh and enliven us. Ziba, the steward of Mephibosheth, brought King David food and wine, the latter to 'refresh those who become exhausted in the desert' (2 Samuel 16:2). Wine does, as the psalmist says, 'gladden the heart of man' (Psalm 104:15).

To ease distress. The writer of Proverbs says that wine is good for those in bitter distress and sorrow in that it helps them to forget their poverty and misery (Proverbs 31:6).

As part of a celebration. The most famous account of the celebratory use of wine is the wedding at Cana, the occasion of Jesus' first miracle (John 2:1–11), but there are numerous other examples of wine being used in celebration.[7] The notion of a future celebration also appears to be present when Jesus tells his disciples at the Last Supper that he will not drink again of the fruit of the vine until he drinks it with them in his Father's kingdom.[8]

As medicine. The physician Luke's account of the good Samaritan says that he 'poured oil and wine' on the wounds of the injured man (Luke 10:34). Often quoted in defence of the use of alcohol is Paul's instruction to Timothy to 'stop drinking only water, and use a little wine because of your stomach and your frequent illness' (1 Timothy 5:23). This is probably as much about avoiding polluted water as about any therapeutic or medicinal value of wine.

As an offering. Drink offerings were required of the Israelites as part of a complex system of offering and sacrifice. Wine was brought as part of the thank-offering of the firstfruits and part of their tithes, as well as for special vows, sacrifices and festival offerings. Though the idea of wine as an offering to God seems out of place to us today, perhaps the principal lesson we can gain from this biblical use of alcohol is that it cannot simply be dismissed as a bad or evil commodity.

Negative comments about alcohol

The Bible also contains a great number of negative references to wine and beer, and almost as many cautionary tales about, and pen-pictures of, those who drink too much. As well as the specific warnings in Proverbs and Isaiah, there are direct instructions in several places in the New Testament not to get drunk on wine (*e.g.* Ephesians 5:18; Romans 13:13) or not to indulge in or be addicted to much wine (*e.g.* 1 Timothy 3:8; Titus 2:3). The use of wine or alcohol itself is not debarred, only drinking to excess, be it drunkenness or an addiction to drink. There are good reasons for this.

First, *alcohol disinhibits our behaviour.* Isaiah refers to those who 'stay up late at night till they are inflamed with wine' (Isaiah 5:11). There are a number of examples in which alcohol causes people to sin or to act in ways that diverge from God's plan. Noah, that righteous man chosen to survive the flood, cultivated a vineyard and subsequently exposed himself while drunk (Genesis 9:20–23). Lot's daughters used the disinhibiting effects of alcohol as a means of getting their father to commit incest with them (Genesis 19:30–38). David was unsuccessful in his attempt to use alcohol as a way of weakening Uriah's vow of temporary celibacy and loyalty to his king and comrades (2 Samuel 11:13).

Secondly, *alcohol impairs our judgment and affects what we say.* When drunk or under the influence of alcohol, we can say and do things that are at best ill-judged and at worst sinful. Isaiah speaks sarcastically about those people who are heroes of the wine bottle (Isaiah 5:22). Herod's rash promise to Salome was almost certainly made while he was drunk, and Xerxes ended up being persuaded to divorce his wife Vashti as a result of his actions when drunk (Esther 1:10 –

2:4). As the book of Proverbs points out, 'Wine is a mocker and beer a brawler; whoever is led astray by them is not wise' (20:1). Even clearer is Isaiah's description of individuals being 'befuddled with wine' (Isaiah 28:7). A refusal to drink excessively is commended, particularly to those in authority: 'Kings should not drink wine or have a craving for alcohol. When they drink, they forget the laws and ignore the rights of people in need' (Proverbs 31:4, Good News Bible).

Thirdly, alcohol lowers our defences, making us vulnerable and unprepared. There are a number of stories in the Bible of people who are drunk and unable to prevent the plots and plans of others against them. Absalom avenged his sister's rape by murdering Amnon when he was drunk (2 Samuel 13:28–29); King Elah was also murdered while drunk (1 Kings 16:9–10). The idea of wine as something that ensnares us is captured by the words of the prophet Nahum: 'They will be entangled among thorns and drunk from their wine; they will be consumed like dry stubble' (Nahum 1:10).

Jesus and alcohol

We know relatively little about Jesus' views on alcohol. Inevitably this has given scope for some individual commentators to interpret his behaviour to mean whatever they want it to mean: either to justify the use of alcohol or to support abstention. Some of this debate has centred on the precise meaning of the word *oinos*, which appears to refer to both wine and grape juice. The argument is whether this was fermented or unfermented. *Oinos* is the wine at the wedding at Cana, where Jesus' first miracle took place. But did it involve the production of an alcoholic drink, or of a pleasant grape juice? Those who see alcohol as only harmful argue that Jesus would not create something that would cause harm and that his miracle must therefore have involved the production of an alcohol-free grape juice. Yet celebrations (both then and now) usually involve alcoholic wine, though the fact that the steward reported that the wine Jesus made was of the best quality does not imply that it was high in alcohol content. As mentioned earlier, there are many examples in the Old Testament of wine being a sign of God's blessing,[9] making Jesus' miracle entirely consistent with this order of creation. In any event, it was not part of Jesus' ministry, or for that matter God's way, to debar us from things which can harm us. As we have seen, drugs as well as other good gifts of God are open to our misuse. We have choice, and free will lies at the centre of God's way with humankind. The argument that Jesus miraculously created a non-alcoholic grape juice to prevent any possible misuse of alcohol is not consistent with the free will that God gives us. It also requires some fairly elastic thinking to make the passage fit with a preconceived notion.

All this, of course, does not necessarily mean that Jesus drank alcoholic wine himself. Perhaps the strongest indication that he did is contained in a story in the Gospels of Matthew and Luke, in which Jesus was commenting upon the negative attitudes of the Pharisees. 'John the Baptist came neither eating bread nor drinking wine, and you say, "He has a demon." The Son of Man came eating and drinking and you say, "Here is a glutton and a drunkard, a friend of tax collectors and 'sinners'"' (Luke 7:33–34; *cf.* Matthew 11:18–19). The Pharisees objected to John's ascetic lifestyle, but they would not accept Jesus' participation in the fun and festivities of the people he mixed with. The behaviour of John and Jesus represented extremes of righteous conduct, useful pegs on which the Pharisees could hang garments of disapproval. Even though the pictures painted by the Pharisees are exaggerations, the fact that John was criticized for abstention seems to imply that Jesus did drink. It seems highly improbable that they would have referred to him as a glutton and a drunkard if his lifestyle had involved total abstinence. That Jesus mixed regularly and easily with people who drank alcohol is beyond doubt, and the balance of probability therefore favours the suggestion that Jesus did drink alcohol.

The final example of Jesus' conduct in relation to alcohol (and indeed other drugs) is his refusal of drugged wine at his crucifixion. Matthew says that it was wine mixed with gall, while Mark refers to wine mingled with myrrh. It has been suggested that the gall may have been extracted from a poppy head, releasing a mild opiate that deadened pain. The painkilling properties of myrrh were among its most valuable uses. What is important, however, is not which painkilling substance Jesus was offered on the cross, but that he refused to take it. This suggests that Jesus knew that he required all his faculties at this, the climax of his purpose on earth. His mind remained focused and unclouded, and if he had been drugged it is unlikely that he would have uttered the words from the cross that he did. We do not know whether he was subjected to extreme temptation and needed a clear head to resist this, whether he wanted his emotions and his perception of his circumstances to be sharp, or if it was simply a question of drinking his cup of suffering to its dregs. What we do know from these accounts is that in this situation he was absolutely clear in his refusal of an emotional, spiritual and physical anaesthetic. Jesus' use of substances was selective, since there were occasions when he drank alcohol and times when he did not. There is a right time and a right place.

The Bible and abstinence

The view that alcohol is seen in the Bible as a normal and acceptable part of life for most people is reinforced by the special circumstances in which abstinence becomes the rule. The Nazirite vow is the most notable example of this. This vow to be 'set apart for God' involved abstaining from fermented drink (or indeed anything coming from the grapevine, including grapes, raisins, grape skins or seeds). Nazirites also vowed not to cut their hair or go near a dead body (see Numbers 6). Samson is perhaps the best-known Nazirite, though infamously he broke his vows regarding contact with a dead body, the cutting of his hair and probably the use of alcohol, if the accounts of his wedding party are anything to go by (see Judges 13 – 16). John the Baptist was another example of someone set aside by God before birth, whose particular ministry meant that he was not to drink any alcohol. The contrast between the working ministries of John and Jesus has already been touched upon, but it is also evident in their pre-birth preparations. God gave Zechariah specific instructions about the requirement for John to abstain from alcohol (Luke 1:15), whereas at the annunciation Mary was given no such instruction for the future lifestyle and ministry of Jesus. In addition to the Nazirites, the Recabites also abstained from alcohol as part of a longstanding family vow of dedication to God made generations before (see Jeremiah 35).[10]

Another situation where use of alcohol was specifically forbidden was when the priests were approaching God in the Tent of Meeting (Leviticus 10:9). What was at stake here was the need for purity, and a conscious mark of honour towards a holy and righteous God. Generations later, Eli the priest showed his concern about this when he rebuked Hannah, who, he believed, was drunk while praying to God outside the temple (1 Samuel 1:9–18).

In a nutshell

The Bible has many things to say about alcohol and its effects. The subject is far more complex than we might wish it to be or than is sometimes suggested. At least three points are clear:

- Alcohol has both benefits and drawbacks. As with most of God's gifts, we can use it or we can abuse it. The devil twists most of God's gifts for his purposes and against the good that God intended in the beginning. Alcohol is no exception.
- Abstinence is not the norm, though individuals may feel called to make a vow of abstinence or decide to abstain from alcohol as an important part of their lifestyle.
- Drunkenness is condemned in both Old and New Testaments.

What these principles might mean in practice will be considered in chapter 8.

chapter

seven

general biblical principles

'There's more evidence to come yet, please your
Majesty,' said the White Rabbit, jumping up in a
great hurry.

The Bible is full of general guidance regarding Christian
conduct, and this inevitably shapes Christians' actions and
attitudes towards drugs. One of its most important teachings
is that Christians are newly created through faith in Jesus
Christ. The picture is presented time and time again,
particularly in the Letters – sometimes in terms of putting on
new clothing, elsewhere as casting off old ways. Christians
are changed people, and this change should be seen in
outward behaviour. Several aspects of Christian character are
relevant to drugs and alcohol.

Self-control

The Bible teaches that self-control is important because of
what we may do when we are not in control. 'Like a city
whose walls are broken down is a man who lacks self-
control,' says the writer of the book of Proverbs (25:28).
Our defences are down and we are vulnerable, not just
physically and emotionally but spiritually. If we are not alert
and self-controlled, we easily fall prey to the temptations of
the devil (1 Peter 5:8), we allow our tongues free reign[1] and

our actions go unchecked. Yet it is not merely the consequences of a lack of self-control that the Bible highlights. Self-control is actually an end in itself, part of the fruit of the Spirit, in marked contrast with the acts of the sinful nature, which include drunkenness and debauchery (Galatians 5:19–24).

Addiction or dependence is marked by a lack of control over a particular behaviour, whether this stems from loss of volition or simply from failure to exercise choice. If we are addicted, we are controlled, even enslaved, by something else, be it alcohol, heroin, gambling or work, since our life is preoccupied by doing or thinking about that thing. Most of us would agree that such addiction or dependence is not good. The majority of people who use drugs and alcohol are not addicted. The issue of self-control is still relevant to them, however, because simply being intoxicated results in a loss of control, albeit temporary. Many people choose to lose self-control on an occasional basis by getting drunk or stoned every now and then. They may see it as a way of switching off at the end of a hard week or after a difficult task is completed; it may be a way of overcoming inhibitions and avoiding responsibility for behaviour, or it may simply be about having a laugh. Outrageous actions or the stupid things said during a night on the town are seen as an important and entertaining part of the activity itself, with stories about people's loss of control surviving long after the events. It is not difficult to see the implications of this for Christians.

Holiness

Holiness is one of the more difficult and perhaps currently unfashionable terms in the Bible. It is nevertheless an important part of the teaching of Scripture from Genesis through to Revelation. Christians are called to be holy in imitation of Jesus (1 Peter 1:15–16), and the church is to be 'a holy nation, a people belonging to God', declaring his praises (1 Peter 2:9). Books have been written about holiness, but essentially it involves being 'set apart' or 'separate'. God is holy, and it is not possible to be both holy and independent of him. Jesus' sacrificial death reconciles us to God and makes holiness a possibility (Hebrews 10:10). The presence of the Holy Spirit within each believer begins the transformation, gradually making us more and more like Jesus and showing us how to lead a life that is both worthy of and pleasing to God. St Paul reminds Christians that our bodies are 'a temple of the Holy Spirit' (1 Corinthians 6:9–20), and that we should therefore honour God with our bodies and minds. Elsewhere in the Bible we are urged to 'offer [our] bodies as living sacrifices, holy and pleasing to God' (Romans 12:1). At the very least, all of this means that we should show respect for our bodies and minds and for the presence of God within us. If we are set apart, we should not be automatically conforming to the ways and patterns of the world around us. 'What agreement is there between the temple of God and idols? For we are the temple of the living God' (2 Corinthians 6:16).

Pleasure-seeking

Closely linked to holiness is the clear injunction that Christians should no longer be concerned with self-interest and pleasure-seeking, but should put God first. Pleasure in itself is not wrong. We can enjoy ourselves, and there is every reason to believe that, as our creator and sustainer, God delights in this, as parents do when their children enjoy things. The problem arises when our search for pleasure impacts upon our relationship with and desire for God, or when it damages and harms us. The western world is given over to immediate gratification, with pleasure an important guiding principle. Its hallmarks are self-indulgence and materialism, which can so easily lead us away from God. Because the use of alcohol and drugs is so often about pleasure-seeking, it is very easy to come to rely upon them to experience pleasure. 'I can have fun only when I'm high.' We need to guard against this attitude. Our pleasures should help us to thank and praise God for his provisions, not replace him in our affections.

Emotions and mood control

Another important drive influencing our use of drugs is the desire to control painful or uncomfortable feelings. God should be at the heart of all that we are, which includes our emotions as much as any other aspect of our lives. The Bible affirms this. 'Cast all your anxiety on him because he cares for you' (1 Peter 5:7), 'Do not let your hearts be troubled and do not be afraid' (John 14:27). It is perhaps no coincidence that taking one day at a time, a central maxim of Alcoholics Anonymous and Narcotics Anonymous, echoes the words of Jesus when he says, 'Do not worry about tomorrow, for tomorrow will worry about itself. Each day has enough trouble of its own' (Matthew 6:34). One of the best-known chapters of the Bible, Psalm 23, is a comfort and source of strength to many people because it reminds us that God is our shepherd, our provider and our constant companion in all circumstances.

None of this is meant to deny or minimize the reality of emotional pain; perhaps for too long, Christian teaching has played it down. Reading about great Christians who struggled with their feelings can help to normalize our own emotional struggles. For example, Martin Luther and Charles Spurgeon endured bouts of severe depression. C. S. Lewis, in *A Grief Observed*, eloquently and with deep feeling recounted his devastating experience of grief. The Bible too can be a great source of encouragement. Though times have changed enormously since its books were written, the human condition has not, and in the Bible we find many deeply human stories of people encountering the unpleasant emotions and feelings that still dominate our lives today. Anxiety, depression, grief, guilt, anger and loneliness are presented not only as emotional burdens that are hard to endure but as spiritual struggles in which God can seem distant or even absent. Stories of Hannah's sadness and grief (1 Samuel 1), Elijah's fear and depression (1 Kings 19), David's guilt (Psalm 51) and Job's emotional battering (in the book that bears his name) not only affirm the reality and intensity of our emotional struggles but offer an assurance that God is in there somewhere, somehow, even though we cannot see him. These people offer us a model because they faced their painful emotions through dialogue with God.

In contrast, modern society offers us analgesics to ease or remove our painful and unpleasant feelings. Legal, illegal and prescribed drugs, as well as food, sex and work, are means by which we sometimes seek to deal with or escape from our feelings. Using drugs to reduce tension or control anxiety is certainly not wrong or bad in itself, but it is risky. It is all too easy to come to depend upon the substance to remove the emotion, rather than see it as enabling us to gain strength to face up to it and wherever possible address its cause. As one psychiatrist put it, 'If you're drinking to relieve an emotion, watch out! If you've got a problem that causes unpleasant emotions, such as anxiety, sort out the problem and then go and have a drink. But if you have a drink to get rid of the emotion, be very, very careful.'[2] When the Bible urges us not to worry about tomorrow, but to hand over our burdens to God, and to rejoice and to trust in him, it does not mean that we should throw away our bandages or dispense with those sources and forms of help and support that are available to us. It simply means that we need to be cautious in attempting to solve our emotional problems without reference to God. Drugs can never be a substitute.

Obeying the law

The Bible instructs Christians to be law-abiding in their behaviour and to 'submit … to the governing authorities' (Romans 13:1). This does not mean that we submit to everything that the state does. What it does mean, is that we obey the laws of our country up to the point at which obedience to the state would entail disobedience to God. At that point our priority is to obey God and to resist the state, but not in a manner that is at odds with our faith. Clearly, this has major implications for the use of drugs that are illegal.

Influencing others

Loving our neighbour is a central requirement of Christian behaviour. The Letters in particular reflect the need to be aware of the ways our behaviour can influence others within the new Christian community. It may be that what we do is not wrong, but it can still be a negative influence on those who are young, weak or impressionable. We need to set a good example to others, irrespective of whether we regard our behaviour as not wrong in itself. In the New Testament this was most clearly seen in the case of Christians who would not eat food offered to idols because they did not want weaker Christians to do the same and feel guilty or troubled as a result (1 Corinthians 8:1–13). We do not want to be a stumbling-block to other Christians, so we must take care about what we do and where we do it. This is a warning that certainly needs to be applied to our use of alcohol and drugs, and interestingly its importance appears to be borne out by current psychological theories of social learning and modelling.[3]

Positive options

Sadly, many people regard Christianity as a set of rules all beginning 'Thou shalt not'. While the Bible does indeed prohibit certain actions and attitudes, its central message is about opening up new possibilities and broadening our horizons rather than reducing or closing them down. It is full of positive messages and options. We can mention five benefits open to us.

First, *God's forgiveness*. Jesus Christ died so that each of us could be forgiven our sin and restored to a whole relationship with God. The Bible teaches that repentance and confession to God are all that we need to receive this forgiveness. We are thus offered a way of dealing with real guilt for the wrongs we have done, and false guilt that arises when we feel bad and worthless. We have an opportunity to make a fresh start.

Secondly, *acceptance*. God loves each one of us with a deep, intimate love. This has profound implications for our lack of self-worth and value. In a world where every one of us so easily falls prey to feeling worthless and unloved, we end up trying to prove ourselves, seeking our identity in what we do, in what we have or through other people's approval of us. God's acceptance is not based upon such transitory human criteria. He loves us, without limit and without end.

Thirdly, *meaning*. We are unique creations, not accidents of nature. Life consists of more than a haphazard series of events involving good or bad fortune. God is present and active in the world, constantly engaged in the work of redemption, creating meaning and wholeness where there appears to be none. He is in the midst of all aspects of our lives – our joys, pains and fears, blessing all our comings and goings.

Fourthly, *hope*. Jesus came to give our lives a hope and a future. If we believe that the creator and sustainer of the universe loves us and cares for us, both now and for eternity, it radically alters the way we view every aspect of our lives. Even death is transformed by this hope, for Christ's death and resurrection mean that, for the believer, this is not the end of existence but the entrance into the presence of God. Here, the Bible tells us, 'there will be no more death or mourning or crying or pain, for the old order of things has passed away' (Revelation 21:4).

Finally, *community*. The kingdom of God is frequently portrayed as a city, a community, even a family, of individuals who are united in their faith and love of God. It is sadly true that the church all too often fails to display the openness, love and forbearance that it is called to show, and which are exemplified in the life of Jesus. Nevertheless, the community of believers still displays something of Christ's message of reconciliation, acceptance and unity through its life together, in marked contrast with the isolation and alienation that are the hallmarks of western societies.

The last two chapters have shown that the Bible provides both specific guidance and general principles that can help to shape Christian conduct in relation to the use of drugs and alcohol. The next chapter will seek to apply these.

chapter

eight

principles and
practicalities

'What am I to do?' exclaimed Alice, looking
about in great perplexity.

In trying to establish an authentic Christian position, it is
important to think about the broad effects and implications
of drug use as well as the specific and general Bible principles
that have already been established. We can summarize these
principles like this:

1. Drunkenness and intoxication are condemned, while
sobriety and temperance (though not necessarily abstinence)
are encouraged.

2. Drugs are a gift from God and in themselves are neither
right nor wrong. It is how they are used that matters. The
same drug can be a valuable aid to our bodily and mental
health or it can be harmful and destructive. Whatever
intrinsic risks there may be in the substances themselves, and
in the ways they are used, the real problems and dangers lie
within each of us and within our society.

3. We are to respect and take good care of our bodies,
since we are all made in God's image. Furthermore, the Spirit
of God lives within each believer. In caring for our bodies,
we should 'nurture and develop them and all their functions
and potentials, to the best of our knowledge and ability. We

should also combat those desires and abstain from those actions that harm, damage or destroy our bodies.'[1] Knowledge and information about the effects of different drugs and routes of administration have improved rapidly over the last hundred years, so that we now know much more about the physical and psychological harm caused.[2] This knowledge supplements biblical warnings about dangers.

4. The reasons for using a drug and the context in which it is used are important. Jesus drank socially with friends and acquaintances, but at his crucifixion, when he most needed his mind and emotions to remain clear, he refused the painkilling sop of drugged wine. This indicates the importance of time and place (what in modern drug parlance is known as the set and setting). It also demonstrates the need to be very careful about how we use or allow drugs to suppress our emotions and feelings or cloud our thoughts and judgments.

5. Principles of Christian living, such as self-control, obeying the law, holiness and the effects of our behaviour on others, all have a considerable bearing on the decisions we make regarding whether or how we use particular drugs.

Having established this biblical framework, it is possible to develop its principles into a series of questions by which we can reflect upon our own use of substances.

How much is too much?

The Bible clearly condemns intoxication and excessive use of alcohol. We can justifiably infer that this applies to other drugs too. Drunkenness and intoxication are not only wrong in themselves, but when we are drunk, stoned or high we are also more likely to fall prey to temptation and sin. We lose control of what we think, do and say. Experience generally confirms this. But if too much of a drug makes us so intoxicated that we lose control, this raises the question, 'How much is too much?'

First, there are certain substances the use of which inevitably results in intoxication. This applies to most hallucinogenic drugs, such as LSD, magic mushrooms and solvents; we are not in control of our thoughts or actions while under their influence.

Secondly, while we may not be intoxicated or completely out of control when under the influence of some drugs, such as amphetamine, cocaine, heroin and Ecstasy, they are substances which have very intense effects. When taken in sufficient quantities they can significantly affect behaviour and actions while the user is under their influence, and self-control is impaired. There are exceptions, such as when amphetamine is used for weight control, or heroin for pain control during childbirth, where the individual would not necessarily be intoxicated or their actions adversely influenced. Generally speaking, however, anyone using these substances recreationally, for 'fun', would be disappointed if they did not experience an intense effect, and most users therefore take enough of the drug to ensure that they do get this effect. For example, many Ecstasy users who begin taking one or two tablets find that their bodies become tolerant of the effects, so if they carry on using the drug regularly, they need to take five or six tablets to get a sufficiently intense experience.[3]

Thirdly, there are a number of drugs that can be used in moderation, to get an effect without necessarily impairing or losing control. Alcohol is a drug that can be used with restraint; indeed, some people who drink take care to ensure that they do not consume enough alcohol to get drunk. Drugs such as cannabis can also be used in a restrained way, as can low doses of prescribed medication such as tranquillizers, antidepressants and minor painkillers. While these substances can be taken in moderation, they can also all be used to a point where the user is no longer in control. Caution needs to be exercised.

Finally, there are a few substances the effects of which do not lead to loss of control, such as nicotine in its various forms of tobacco, and caffeine in tea, coffee and cola drinks.

Is it legal?

Christians are urged to be law-abiding in their behaviour unless there are fundamental reasons for disobeying the law. These are usually situations where a law goes directly against our faith. It is certainly not possible to justify breaking the law on the grounds of pleasure-seeking and enjoyment alone. Christians are to 'shine ... like stars' (Philippians 2:15) as an example to the rest of society. It would not reflect well upon the faith if a Christian were arrested and charged with a criminal offence as a result of using illegal substances.

On the basis of law alone, drugs such as caffeine, solvents, tobacco and alcohol, the selected use of magic mushrooms and the use of drugs prescribed personally would not be excluded. In the UK at least, most other drugs would not pass this test. Given that a state's legal authority comes from God (Romans 13:1–7), Christians should respect the laws of that state. On this basis one would expect Christians in Saudi Arabia to respect Saudi law, which does not permit the use of alcohol. In Holland, the acceptance of cannabis use in coffee shops means that the 'obedience to the law' factor alone would not necessarily exclude Christians from using the drug, though other principles might need to be considered.

What harm can it do?

There are few substances that do not have an effect on our bodies. Over recent years we have become more and more aware of the effects and dangers of the food we eat, the air we breathe and the water we drink. In looking at the harm that a drug does to us, it is important to get a sense of balance, not necessarily avoiding substances simply because there is a risk of some slight harmful effect. Or, if we do, we should be consistent and extend this to other areas of our life such as the foods we eat, our weight, how much we exercise and whether we overwork.

When we look at the harm caused to the body by using a particular drug, we must consider the damage done by the drug itself (its toxicity) and that caused by the way it is used.

Heroin, for example, when taken in moderate doses, causes little harm to the body and is less physically harmful than alcohol, even when both are taken regularly. A quarter of all male hospital admissions in the UK result from alcohol-related health problems. The problems with heroin, however, come from the impurities within the drug, its potential for addiction and the route of administration, particularly injecting. Impurity and adulterants in illegal substances are always a potential source of harm.

Nicotine is usually smoked, a method which will inevitably have a toxic effect upon the body. Cigarette smoke contains over 3,000 chemicals. While a single cigarette will not kill a person, each one adds to the damage being done to the heart, lungs and other organs. It is estimated that on average, each cigarette reduces a smoker's life expectancy by several minutes. Smoking cannabis also carries risks for any users, irrespective of any benefits or relief it might also give. In particular, it causes damage to the lungs. Little research has been carried out into harm caused by oral doses of cannabis, but if taken in standard or controlled amounts this seems likely to be much safer.

The 'harm' and 'reasons for using' principles take us into very murky waters indeed, and we would do well to avoid using them to judge others. Their main value is as a personal check, to help us think about the harm that a substance might do to us and to consider how to minimize these harmful effects. 'As long as we are still in the body, let us care well for our bodies so that we can bring joy and peace of God's kingdom to those we meet on our journey.'[4]

Is it habit-forming?

As we have seen, all substances can be psychologically addictive, but some, such as alcohol, heroin, Valium or tobacco, can be physically addictive too. Certain drugs, such as heroin, nicotine and crack, are also more likely to lead to dependency than others. Although it is possible to use any drugs without becoming addicted or dependent upon them, we must be very wary indeed, even if they are legal, because using them exposes us to the possibility of developing a dependency.[5] This may be a risk that is not worth taking. As one anti-smoking campaign used to put it, 'the best way to stop smoking is never to start'.

It is helpful to set limits on our own use of drugs by thinking about how often we are using a particular substance and whether we can do without it. Ensuring that there are periods of time when we go without the drug is a good way of minimizing the risk of developing a physical or emotional dependency upon it.

Why do we use it?

As we have seen, people have many reasons for using drugs: pleasure, pain relief, alleviation of emotional problems, escape, sociability, and so on. Our use in itself may not be sinful, but simply a way of coping with the consequences of our own and human sin, together with the shortcomings of the fallen world in which we live. Pleasure and sociability are certainly not wrong in themselves, but, as we saw earlier, if we use a particular substance to get these effects, there is always a risk that we may start to need the drug in order to have fun or to be sociable. The use of drugs to avoid unpleasant feelings is more complex and touches upon a deeper human and societal need. Legal, illegal and many mood-altering prescribed drugs are used for this purpose. We live in a quick-fix society. 'Our first reaction to emotional discomfort is often to avoid it, distance it or run. Jesus showed that pain has to be withstood and borne. Without it there is no resurrection.'[6] In reflecting upon whether we ought to be using drugs, it is important to try and take an honest look at why we are doing so and, again, to start with ourselves rather than others.

How does my use affect others?

We need to ask ourselves two questions about the way our use of substances might affect other people.

First, does my use affect others directly? In the case of

smoking, for example, evidence suggests that it has damaging effects on the health of others nearby (passive smoking). It is important to show respect for others and for their health. Another example is drinking and driving. We may drink and drive and remain within the legal limits. Although we may not be breaking the law, are we showing proper responsibility for the well-being of others? Any amount of alcohol affects driving skills. Drivers with blood alcohol levels just *below* the legal limit are up to four times more likely to have an accident than if they had not been drinking.[7] It has been estimated that in the UK, 1600 road accidents and 110 deaths per year could be avoided if people using prescribed tranquillizers did not drive.[8] As Christians, we need to be responsible in our use of all substances.

Secondly, what example does our use set for younger or more impressionable people? Christians are to be careful about their behaviour so as not to adversely influence new Christians or weaker individuals who may copy them (1 Corinthians 8:1–13). We may feel that using a particular drug is OK for us, but others may take this as an indication that it is normal or acceptable conduct for them too. This might cause them problems. Sensitivity to the needs and circumstances of others is an important guiding principle. We must also think about our attitude to medicines and the sort of example this gives, particularly to children. As Sister Alison Mary observes, 'we tend to take it for granted that our doctor ought to dish out pills for us; that we need an aspirin for only a slight headache or a sleeping tablet for only a few hours wakefulness. Christians could do much by reverencing the natural resources of their physical make-up and only resort to medicines for necessary reasons.'[9] We need to plan how and when we use drugs and alcohol and what controls and boundaries we need to put in place.

Avoiding gnats and camels

All too often, human opinions and biblical interpretation are given the status of divine imperatives. Rules are made which become legalistic and rigid. In a blistering attack upon the religious leaders of his time, Jesus condemned them for being so concerned with observing the external niceties of the law that they forgot the principles that lay behind it – justice, mercy and faithfulness. They were so busy straining out the gnats that they ended up swallowing camels (Matthew 23:24). Fortunately, we are saved through grace, not through law. The questions posed in this chapter offer a possible template against which we can determine our own conduct in relation to drugs. They are for reflection about our use of substances rather than rules by which we judge the conduct of others or make ourselves feel good by comparison. The fourth of the twelve steps of the Alcoholics Anonymous programme states the need to make 'a searching and fearless moral inventory of ourselves'.[10] Adam and Eve hid from God when they sinned, and did not want him to see what they had done. It is essential that we are open and honest in asking God to help and guide us in what we do or don't do with drugs. We would, however, do well to echo the words of the psalmist: 'Search me, O God, and know my heart; test me and know my anxious thoughts. See if there is any offensive way in me, and lead me in the way everlasting' (Psalm 139:23–24).

part **three**

drugs, christians and society

chapter nine

inside the gates of eden

> Alice opened the door and found that it led into
> a small passage, not much larger than a rat-
> hole: she knelt down and looked along the
> passage into the loveliest garden you ever saw.
> How she longed to get out of that dark hall and
> wander about among those beds of bright
> flowers and those cool fountains.

Within each of us there remains a deep, unconscious longing
for completeness and perfection. The Bible account of the
Garden of Eden shows that this longing is extremely
significant. We are spiritual creatures made to live in
harmony with God, with one another and with the rest of
creation, a unity that was lost through sin. We have been
trying to find our way back to Eden ever since. There is a
desire for something more substantial and meaningful in life;
we sense that something is missing or things are not as they
should be, even if we cannot put our finger on what is
wrong. Paul Tournier calls it 'a muffled discontent with
ourselves, a distress of which we are not always aware'.[1] The
singer Sinead O'Connor observed that 'as a race we feel
empty', while Prince Charles is reported as saying that 'there
remains deep in the soul a persistent and unconscious anxiety
that something is missing, some ingredient that makes life
worth living'.[2] Bishop Richard Holloway paints a more

mystical picture: 'In some mysterious sense we are all cast out of a homeland. We are all in a far country, cut off from a joy we have never yet known, yet born somehow remembering.'[3] The early 1970s song 'Woodstock', with its urge 'to get ourselves back to the Garden', was merely restating the case. Echoes of Eden resonate in the collective unconscious.

Drugs appear to meet our deep spiritual need in at least three ways.

A route to God

'I'll die young but it's like kissing God,' said comedian Lenny Bruce about his use of drugs. It was not a new idea. Drugs have been seen as a means of transcendence and getting closer to God for as long as we can trace. In Ancient Greece, the priestess of the Oracle at Delphi is thought to have inhaled carbon dioxide fumes escaping from the rocks to provide visions and assist in making prophecies. The peyote cactus was an integral part of the religious worship of both the Aztecs and the North American Indians. Indian Brahmin priests have used cannabis to help them in their meditations for hundreds of years, and, much more recently, the self-same cannabis, referred to as ganja or 'the herb', has become intrinsically associated with Rastafarianism. Apart from these and many other uses of drugs by institutional religions, individuals also use them for private experiences of transcendence. The poet Coleridge said that laudanum gave him a sense of divine repose, 'a spot of enchantment, a green place of fountain and flowers and trees, and these in the very heart of a waste of sands'.[4] At the turn of the century, the psychologist William James commented on people whose knowledge of God had appeared to deepen through the use of gases such as nitrous oxide and chloroform. In the 1960s, LSD became the best-known vehicle for such experiences. *Time-Life* chairman Henry Luce said that through using LSD he had glimpsed God. More recently, another user, writing on the internet, said, 'I never had any bad LSD. I saw God regularly, every Saturday afternoon for two years.' Cannabis, Ecstasy, cocaine, heroin, magic mushrooms and mescaline have all been used to gain transcendent experiences. 'Above us the vaulted sky arched like a cathedral, sprinkled with stars. Everything inside me felt like an offering to some unseen but benevolent presence.'[5] This 'urge to transcend self-conscious self-hood is a principal appetite of the soul', according to Aldous Huxley.[6]

Personal fulfilment and meaning

Many people feel that drug use fulfils them; they seem more truly themselves. 'It makes me feel fully alive,' one amphetamine user said. Another reported that 'on E I felt I had developed and matured mentally and didn't feel such a fickle and shallow person any more. I can honestly say that I am a better person from having taken Ecstasy.'[7] LSD is also a drug with introspective tendencies that gives many who use it a feeling of insight and self-understanding. In the 1960s Paul McCartney said that 'it opened my eyes. It made me a better, more honest, more tolerant member of society.'[8] 'I became a real person,' another user said, while Hollywood legend Cary Grant declared that LSD made him feel 'born again' following a period of depression. His choice of words is interesting, but, given the 'spiritual' significance of drug use, it is perhaps not surprising that people sometimes use religious terminology to describe their experiences.

It is not just hallucinogenic drugs that give this sense of fulfilment. Heroin users also speak in this way. 'I felt like I'd come home at last.' 'I'd found what I was looking for all my life.' 'It makes me feel that I belong.' These are typical comments. For some people, drugs offer a profound experience of finding something they had been looking for. Many personal poems written about drugs refer to a homecoming or allude to the discovery of a long-lost lover whom they had been seeking. Again, there are clearly similarities with the language of evangelical Christianity.

A sense of community

Drug use has always been associated with a sense of unity

among users. There is the obvious unity that arises from the shared activity: drinkers at the pub, smokers on the office doorstep, young people sniffing gas together. This sort of unity is no different from that found in any group that shares an activity, whether caravan owners, gardeners or joggers. The effects of the drugs themselves, however, can also bring feelings of unity and community. In part this may result from the breaking down of inhibitions, but there does appear to be something more than this with certain substances. Sitting with a group of friends, smoking cannabis and listening to music has been as much about a harmonious communal activity as about an individual drug experience. Over thirty years ago, a mother described the experiences of her divided and dysfunctional family when her son persuaded them to smoke cannabis together. 'It was really marvellous. Everyone managed to talk together; there was no tendency to put anyone down ... The family that night was closer than any time I can recall ... We were all very happy together and went off to our rooms feeling as if we loved each other for the human beings we were, not for mere points on a scale of achievement.'[9] In the last couple of decades, many of the newer generation of drug users have found even more intense communal bonding in Ecstasy experiences. It is no coincidence that two of the early popular names for Ecstasy were 'Adam' and 'Eve', harking back to the Garden of Eden once again. For many, using E is a profound experience. 'Nothing compares to the unity of ravers. We are a true community.'[10] 'Here there's a real sense of belonging, of community. Why can't it always be like this?'[11]

We still haven't found what we're looking for

There can be no doubt that drugs do provide many people with a sense of 'otherness', something that is both bigger and more important than anything else they have previously encountered. They are unquestionably a spiritual experience. Yet despite the optimistic fanfare, there are a number of reasons that drugs do not provide the ultimate spiritual answers that we are looking for.

Drug experiences are only a perception of reality

Drug effects are to do with the substance, the user and his or her situation and mood rather than with inner transcendence or absolute meanings. Drugs introduce new chemicals into our brains or induce them to release natural chemicals such as serotonin or endorphins that may feel pleasant or distort our perception of the ordinary, but 'we should question whether visionary experiences are contained in a few simple molecules'.[12] Even the late Nicholas Saunders, known as the 'Buddha of Euphoria' because of his interest in and advocacy of Ecstasy, seems to accept the chemistry involved. 'Always remember that the bad experience is the effect of a chemical. The same chemical can produce beautiful effects.'[13] While we may not wish to view drug experiences as nonsense, like dreams they are usually non-sense in that it is difficult to make any sense of them. Meanings tend to be constructed afterwards, when the user is 'straight', in an attempt to make sense of the memories and experiences. As such, they are entirely a matter of interpretation, and totally subjective.

Drugs do not provide a permanent answer

However profound the drug experience may be, in order to replicate it, ever more of the substance must be taken. Re-experiencing the first occasion can be permanently elusive, but even if good experiences are repeatedly achieved, they can still begin to wear thin eventually. As one Ecstasy user said, 'Personally, I'm bored with feeling so nice every Saturday evening.'[14] 'Eternal well-being on a Saturday night is, it would seem, hard to sustain.'[15] Things also change as a result of taking more of the drug, with physical and psychological needs taking precedence over anything else. When the shadowy parts of our minds come out to haunt us, visions of hell can be just as common as visions of heaven. Sometimes the restless, hungry feelings that we are trying to escape reappear. 'Everything was brilliant ... Then it just went downhill. Everyone was moaning when they were coming down, you were depressed and you were sitting there wondering what to do.'[16] The hollow feeling inside continues to grow, as the Pulp song 'Sorted for E's and Whizz' acknowledges. The things we are looking for or thought we had found in a drug, be they feelings, mood or a sense of the divine, remain beyond our grasp.

Drugs change how we feel, not what we are

The changes induced by drugs are not only transient but superficial, because they do not actually change us inwardly. Take away the drug and we are more or less back to where we started. The musician Brian Eno commented upon this: 'I get thoroughly fed up with hearing about people's mystical drug experiences. I don't see the experiences doing anything. I know people who've been having sublime experiences on drugs for years and they're still the same people. It doesn't seem to have affected their behaviour in any way.'[17]

Some drugs do induce a temporary sense of sharing and camaraderie, but often this has more to do with the perceptual distortion induced by the drug than with any real change or difference in the people themselves. As we know only too well with alcohol, the sense of unity brought about by drinking can rapidly switch to violence and aggression. The unity of a group of cannabis users has a great deal to do with a perception of sharing rather than with any real unity of mind and spirit, as those who have spent time with a group of dope smokers without having a smoke themselves will testify. Even Ecstasy use does not guarantee an invitation to the shared experience, as C. J. Stone discovered: 'At times I would find myself in situations where I was simply out of place, surrounded by wealthy hedonists and bored looking young model girls who wouldn't give me a second glance. I began to recognise the drawbacks to the party scene ... over-priced drugs and undervalued humanity. That gorgeous unity was available only to those who could afford to pay.'[18]

Finding God, finding ourselves

Transcendence, fulfilment and community are all part of God's blueprint for us. As St Augustine said, addressing God: 'Thou hast made us for thyself, and our hearts are restless till they find their rest in thee.' We are orphans, and, in our restless search for him, 'fatal substitutes abound'.[19] Some of these substitutes, such as drugs, alcohol and gambling, are condemned by society when used excessively, but there are many others that can be just as spiritually fatal in excess, but which are loudly applauded. Work, money, fitness and consumerism can all become substitutes for our true calling and identity. Sadly, people addicted to drugs or alcohol are often offered the latter substitutes as apparently worthwhile replacements or goals to give their lives new meaning and purpose. As a result it is not uncommon to see one tyranny replaced by another. Renton, the heroin-using anti-hero of the film *Trainspotting*, could see this when he railed against consumerism, with its 'cars, compact-disc players and electrical tin-openers', 'mind-numbing, spirit-crushing game shows', 'three-piece suites in a range of fabrics, matching luggage and Saturday morning DIY'. 'Choose life.' If that is life, no wonder he and many others choose something else.

Drugs offer spiritual promises that they cannot deliver. There are no backstage passes into the presence of God, though his grace is such that there may have been instances where he has worked through drug experiences to reveal himself and touch people's lives.[20] The litmus test of this is how far these experiences point people to the truth. Jesus said, 'I am the way, the truth and the life. Nobody comes to the Father except through me' (John 14:6). God meets us where we are, without special techniques or rituals and without the need for mind-altering substances. But we must look for him. Honesty, persistence and a willingness to follow where the road leads are part of this search. Above all, it is a journey of the heart (Jeremiah 29:13) rather than a trip for our senses.

The longing for community, writes Henri Nouwen, 'is a God-given desire, a desire that causes immense pain as well as immense joy. Jesus came to proclaim that our desire for communion is not in vain but will be fulfilled by the one who gave us that desire. The passing hints of communion are only hints of the communion that God has promised us.'[21] Finding God goes hand in hand with finding satisfaction and true fulfilment. In a series of declarations about himself, Jesus stated that he is the only way to God and the only way we can find satisfaction, understanding and meaning. He satisfies our hunger and quenches our thirst (John 6:35), he rescues us from darkness and confusion and gives us light (John 8:12), he acknowledges our worth, significance and value as creatures made in the image of God. We are loved by God and he is constantly at work renewing, redeeming and restoring us to the wholeness he intended from the beginning.

Hints of glory

While drugs may fail to provide long-term, satisfying answers to questions about our identity and the purpose of life, hints of glory remain. The human search for meaning and the need to worship and build our lives around something or someone can be seen. As John Smith has observed, even in idolatry there are signs of hope because people are still searching, still longing for that greater and bigger love. But drugs and alcohol, like possessions, sex, work or religious legalism, will all betray us if we place our trust in them. The answer does not lie in any of these 'substitutes'. The community of the rave, the glimpse of the divine and the sense of the eternal that substance use can bring are merely hints of glory. 'They are not the thing itself, they are only the scent of a flower we have not yet found, the echo of a tune we have not yet heard, news of a country we have not yet visited.'[22]

ten

wake-up call

> 'The Dormouse is asleep again,' said the Hatter,
> and he poured a little hot tea upon its nose.

The church's response to the use of alcohol and drugs has been patchy. Interest in the subject has ebbed and flowed, with most of the practical outworking of faith left to individual Christians acting alone or in small groups with other committed people, believers and non-believers. A reflection on the church's past involvement with drugs and alcohol and a look at where it stands in the present can provide some useful pointers to where it should be seeking to go in the future and how it might go about this.

Past shortcomings

The history of the British temperance movement, especially the role of the Church of England in it, has much to teach us today. The temperance movement is often seen as a prime example of a Christian crusade promoting upright and sober behaviour. It is certainly true that Christians, particularly nonconformists, were involved with the temperance movement from its earliest beginnings, but in fact it was far more closely connected with secular parties, particularly in the early period of its life. 'Chartists and radicals, sceptics and rationalists often found teetotalism easier to accept than did traditional Christians, whether Wesleyan Methodists or high or low Anglicans.'[1] To this extent it was similar to some of the other great campaigns of the last couple of centuries such as the anti-slavery movement, welfare reform or the Campaign for Nuclear Disarmament, where secular groups and individual Christians have worked alongside one another, united by a common cause.

Within the temperance movement, there were two main strands of thinking. Some believed that the state should intervene, and pressed for legislation to control the availability of alcohol. In the United States this ultimately led to prohibition.[2] Within the British temperance movement however, moral education was favoured as the way to change people's thinking and drinking. Organizations such as the National Temperance League and the Band of Hope devoted considerable time, energy and ingenuity to educating the young about the evils of drink. Lantern slides, songs and programmes of physical activity and exercise were used to good effect. There are parallels between these activities and today's drug education programmes. Their approach is also relevant to the broader debate about whether the state should control the availability of substances or whether their use is a matter of personal choice and responsibility.

In the first half of the nineteenth century, the Church of England actually worked against the goal of abstinence, influenced mainly by the views of the medical profession. Most doctors and physicians believed that alcohol was an essential food and medicine,[3] and the clergy largely accepted this. Some interesting comments from that period remain. A Manchester priest wrote that at his ordination he was advised by an 'excellent clergyman' to 'get your warden to let you have a bottle of wine in the vestry, and when you go to change your surplice for your gown, always take a glass'. The Revd Henry Moule recorded that without two glasses of wine he could not get through his Sunday duties. Such views were not uncommon.[4] One clergyman, Henry Ellison, initially tried teetotalism but felt that it enfeebled his constitution, necessitating two or three glasses of wine a day to maintain his health (although he later became a prominent Anglican temperance campaigner).[5] Some who gave up drinking reported that after stopping they felt unwell, but were restored to full health when they began to drink again. This reinforced the belief that alcohol was a medically valuable substance, whereas in fact they may well have been experiencing symptoms resulting from a physical or psychological dependence.

As medical opinion began to change through the middle of the nineteenth century, so the position of many Anglican leaders began to change too. Double standards about who should use alcohol remained, reflected in the paternalistic attitude towards the working classes, who were believed to be in particular need of moral protection from the evils of alcohol and drunkenness. It was only when teetotalism became more acceptable among the upper classes of society that the shift in attitudes was complete. By 1900 half the Anglican bishops were teetotal.[6] With the exception of a few notable individuals among its ranks, the public voice of the established church in England had been confused or silent during much of the temperance debate. Instead of being a visionary leader, it had been a reluctant follower, allowing louder voices and different values to shape society's response.

Looking at the temperance movement in England provides a single snapshot of a much larger historical scene. The most inspiring examples of Christian involvement with drugs and alcohol have been in practical care and concern rather than in moral campaigns. Individual Christians and churches, fired by their faith, began some of the first programmes of support and rehabilitation for those with severe alcohol and drug problems. Organizations such as the Salvation Army, the Church Army, the London Embankment Mission and others started this work in the nineteenth century, providing food, clothing and shelter for those living rough on the streets, usually as a consequence of severe alcohol problems.

Alcohol remained the principal drug of use and misuse in the UK during the first half of the twentieth century, with the established organizations continuing to work in a quiet, undramatic way. With the growth of youth culture and the rise in drug use during the 1960s, those involved with young people began to see the damaging effects of certain substances, particularly amphetamine and heroin. This 'new' group of users did not fit into existing services for those with alcohol problems, and as a result their needs went largely unmet. Aware of this in a way that the authorities were not, a number of individual Christians, working alone or in small pressure-groups, set about doing something to improve the provision of services. The commitment and involvement of these individuals were passionate and total. Providing direct care and support, and also by campaigning and lobbying, they managed to help establish services, umbrella organizations and policy groups that have left their mark on the scene today. London was a particular focus, with Kenneth Leech's work at St Anne's in Soho the best-known example. Others, such as the rehabilitation provided by a community of nuns at Spelthorne St Mary, and the Coke Hole Trust in Andover, set the benchmarks for residential services that followed later. Thirty years on, the Coke Hole Trust continues to provide a high-quality rehabilitation programme.

There are now over seventy drug and alcohol treatment centres around the UK.[7] Many are secular and offer no spiritual input, but Christian organizations such as Teen Challenge, Yeldall Manor, Hebron House and Meta House employ Christian staff and offer a variety of help and treatment interventions. The Church of Scotland has also been at the forefront of Christian care for many years, and is Scotland's largest voluntary-sector social-work employer. As well as providing residential treatment and rehabilitation centres, such as Rainbow House and Malta House, it has also been involved with important work in the community, such as day centres, supported accommodation, counselling services and outreach work with drug-using prostitutes.

One of the most remarkable Christian drug projects in Britain is Kaleidoscope, whose inspirational story shows how local churches and individual Christians can make a significant difference.[8] Beginning in the late 1960s, the John Bunyan Baptist Church in Kingston-upon-Thames, under the leadership of its minister Eric Blakebrough, sought to work with the local young people, many of whom were living in squats and heavily involved in drug use. Gradually the youth club was transformed into a place where young people could meet in safety with their needs as the priority. An all-night drop-in on Fridays, offering food, medical support and a general atmosphere of love and acceptance, attracted dozens of young people through its doors. When the numbers and need outstripped the limited space, the small church took the bold decision to demolish the church building, sell off some of the site and use the proceeds and other assets to build a new club, a hostel and a smaller church building. Today, through setbacks and triumphs, it is thriving and still working on the front line where people are at most risk and in greatest need.

Present achievements

After the 1960s and '70s, when Christians had begun to engage with the issue of drugs, things quietened down for a time. New social challenges arose, such as the environment, abortion, HIV and Aids, and attention moved away from substance use and misuse. The existing specialist Christian sector carried on doing what it did best, usually operating within an abstinence framework, while the majority of substance-misuse problems were picked up by the secular services of the statutory and voluntary sectors.

In the late 1980s, in the wake of public health concern about HIV and hepatitis, the dominant treatment principle of abstinence began to play second fiddle to harm reduction, which seeks to minimize the harm of continued drug use and sexual behaviour.[9] This created dilemmas for many agencies and individuals, particularly Christians, since it appeared to muddy the waters about acceptable and unacceptable drug use and practices. In fact, the waters always were murky, particularly regarding legal and prescribed substances. Harm reduction proved to be less of a problem to organizations providing residential treatment where abstinence remained the rule, but Christians working in the community and out on the streets have had to engage with and operate within or at least alongside a harm-reduction philosophy. The success and credibility of agencies such as Kaleidoscope, St Luke's in Dagenham or Simpson House in Edinburgh, as well as much detached youth work, shows that Christian involvement in this area is not only possible but vital, since the vast majority of problem drinkers and drug users will always be within our local communities where such agencies work.

Over recent years there has been a reawakening of the 1960s' concern about the problems of drugs and alcohol in local communities. Nationally, the Evangelical Alliance set up the Evangelical Coalition on Drugs (ECOD) an interest group of around 200 individuals and organizations. Although this represents only one Christian perspective on drugs, it is the strongest collective Christian voice currently to be heard in the UK.

There has recently been some discussion at denominational level too. A study group of the Church of Scotland has looked at issues surrounding the decriminalization of drugs, while its General Assembly regularly considers both the theology and the social-care issues surrounding drugs and alcohol. The Methodist Conference has also considered important areas concerned with both alcohol and drugs over the last few years, and in 1998 the Church of England debated the misuse of drugs in the General Synod for the first time in its history. At this stage it is difficult to tell whether these or other church discussions and debates on drugs will prove to be anything more than a fleeting interest in a topical issue, a new 'dish of the day' on the menu of social responsibility.

At a local level, however, where the real marks of mission must always be worked out, it is encouraging and exciting to see an increasing number of individual Christians or small Christian groups developing and contributing towards local drug initiatives. Unfortunately, they still remain the concern of a small number of committed individuals, 'product champions', rather than something that is acknowledged or made a priority by the wider church membership. Ultimately, the key to serious intent in confronting the problems of alcohol and drugs, and indeed the addictive society in which we live, lies in ownership of the problem by all Christians

Whatever individual Christians may be doing on the ground, or churches discussing behind closed doors, Christian voices and that of the church appear to be largely silent in political and public debates on drugs and alcohol. The 1998 government White Paper *Tackling Drugs to Build a Better Britain* presents a ten-year strategy for combating drug misuse, yet makes no mention of the role of the church or indeed of the spiritual significance of drug use. Responsibility for this omission lies with the church. As was the case with the temperance movement, Christians are failing to shape the course of events in society, and without their unique perspective the picture will be incomplete. It is vital that Christians should be at the heart of the local and national debate about drugs and alcohol as leaders and partners, not as followers or silent onlookers. To do this it is not good enough simply to follow the views and received wisdom of others, whether the medical profession, politicians, the Moral Majority or anyone else who talks loudly enough. We must have our own ideas, using our minds to think through what we believe and why. Once clear about a Christian position, we need to express this perspective explicitly and repeatedly, in the right places, drawing on the experiences of the local Christian groups and churches who are listening to those in need and working with them at ground level.

How we do this and what we offer are even more important than the message itself. We shall be known by our deeds and by our conduct. When those with drink or drug problems or a history of difficulties can sit in our churches and be accepted for the people they are, rather than being defined by their problems, we shall be on the way. It is not easy, and never comfortable. But if we are to be God's new community, offering signposts to better things, reflecting the heart of God is not an optional extra but the defining characteristic of our activity.

eleven

a shot of love

> 'The game's going on rather better now,' she
> said, by way of keeping up the conversation a
> little.
>
> ''Tis so,' said the Duchess: 'and the moral of
> that is – "Oh 'tis love, 'tis love, that makes the
> world go round!"'

Love is at the heart of our calling, if we are to reflect the character and concerns of God to the world and the individuals in it. God is love. Each of us was created by love and for love, and only through love will we find true fulfilment. Love is not about feelings or giving things, which our materialistic society invariably confuses with love. Love is about self-giving, and any practical thing we do or give is an expression of that self-giving. The absence of love is the root of many of society's problems, but where it is present it can be world-changing, as the life of Jesus showed. His love 'conquered the great divide', and risky, self-giving love can still break through today. Mother Theresa's life and work were suffused with a love that sent ripples around the world. She was clear about the problem:

> The biggest disease today is not leprosy or tuberculosis, but rather the feeling of being unwanted, uncared for and deserted by everybody. The greatest evil is the lack

of love and charity, the terrible indifference towards one's neighbour who lives at the roadside assaulted by exploitation, corruption, poverty and disease.[1]

Despair, hopelessness and chronically low self-esteem exist deep within our own society, and are hallmarks borne by many people who use drugs and alcohol heavily. Bob Dylan sang that he did not need a shot of heroin or a shot of codeine, or even a shot of whisky, but 'a shot of love'. Fundamental beliefs and divine characteristics underpin the love that we give.

Made in the image of God

Every person is unique and of infinite value because he or she is made in the image of God. Those who have problems with drugs and alcohol are people, not 'addicts' who are defined by their particular circumstances. Labels such as 'the deaf', 'the disabled', 'HIV sufferers' and 'junkies' all create unhelpful and often painful divisions between 'them' and 'us'. Labels not only stigmatize but serve to obscure the individual's humanity and unity with the rest of us. Ironically, the experience of powerlessness and struggle makes many such 'ordinary' people more fully human and alive, as Bill Kirkpatrick illustrates so powerfully in his remarkable book *Cry Love, Cry Hope*.[2] Malcolm Muggeridge noticed this too in the work of the Missionaries of Charity: 'These lepers and little children that you get off the street, they're not just destitute people to be pitied, they're marvellous people.'[3] This is the experience of those who work with the poor and needy: those we seek to love and serve give us back, out of their poverty, far more than we give to them. Whether we see this or not, whether we are accepted or rejected, people still matter. Each one of us, though fallen, has infinite worth as a human being made in God's likeness, with unique capacities; and this should always be reflected in our relationship with others. As Kenneth Leech says, this means that while 'the use of drugs raises specific questions and problems, Christian ministry is to all people'.[4]

Grace and mercy

Grace, mercy and a non-judgmental spirit are not just good counselling theory or even part of the common sense needed to help us build healthy, respectful relationships with other people. They are sound theology. God's grace is freely given to each of us.

In the kingdom of God, there is no place for pride or for first- and second-class citizens, because we are all equally dependent upon grace. God loves the injecting drug user every bit as much as he loves the evangelistic preacher, while the charismatic house-church leader's need of God's mercy is just as great as that of the worst drunk. 'All have sinned and fall short of the glory of God' (Romans 3:23), and there is none among us who can work our own passage into God's favour.

In earlier chapters, I have stressed the need to apply Bible principles and guidelines to our own lives rather than using them as a measure to gauge others. We should always remember where we have come from. At the foot of the cross we are all guilty and in need of mercy. Working through the twelve steps of the Alcoholics Anonymous programme constantly reminds people of what they have done, where they have been and their daily need for grace and mercy.

As new Christians, we know this well, but with time we can easily forget and become proud and legalistic, what John Smith has referred to as 'being uppity'.[5] Many of our church fellowships and house-groups could do with a good deal more of the honesty and candour of Alcoholics Anonymous and Narcotics Anonymous meetings. Grace is freely given, and that is all we ever have. 'If we allow ourselves to join the bystanders muttering at the promiscuity of the woman taken in adultery,' writes Sheila Cassidy, 'we will, sure as eggs, find that it is our darkest, dirtiest secrets that are being written in the dust for all to see.'[6] Jesus did not condemn the woman. Our theology of drug use cannot involve judging and condemning others.

Justice

God is a God of justice, and requires justice not only among his own people but also within each nation and community. The book of Amos hammers this message home: God hates oppression and exploitation; prosperity brings responsibility towards the disadvantaged; worship accompanied by social injustice or indifference to those in need is unacceptable to God. It is not hard to apply these principles to the field of drugs and alcohol, where exploitation and injustice are rife in our own communities, our country and in our relationships with other nations. This may require us to take a more political stance than we have done, or to become involved in advocacy for the powerless. We need to be sensitive to and aware of the whole range of injustices, and to build principles of justice into our responses.

Truth

It is essential that we seek to represent the truth in all that we do. Drugs are scary things for many people, particularly parents of teenagers; and if the church is to speak about drugs it must be honest and avoid gratuitously feeding on people's fears. We can do this only if we are accurately informed ourselves. Some Christian books are guilty of a sensationalism that seems to parallel that of some tabloid newspapers. For example, one recent British book for parents started by giving an account of a young man who had murdered his parents while using a drug called PCP. Not only was this a secondhand story from the United States, but it was about a drug rarely (if ever) seen in the UK. Sensationalism must be avoided, especially stories from other contexts. We do not need to distort or to be economical with the truth. 'A truthful witness does not deceive,' according to the book of Proverbs (14:5).

We must be truthful and honest in our dealings with every aspect of the problem: honest and courageous enough to speak out about the economic and structural reasons for drug and alcohol use, about the personal and social factors that contribute to the problem, and about the spiritual dimension too. It is also important to be honest about the consequences for others of dependent drug use – neglect, fear, crime, health risks and so on. Where wrongs are being done, we do not represent the truth if we collude with them. Love and justice come into play here too.

Christians believe that Jesus Christ personified the truth. He is, in his own words, 'the way and the truth and the life' (John 14:6). This is the truth that we seek to share because it offers us a new way of life that is truly liberating and fulfilling. Even here the need for truthfulness is paramount. Some 1960s evangelists, desperate to communicate with a younger generation who were disillusioned by straight society, declared that 'Jesus is the best fix' and exhorted young people to 'turn on to Jesus'. But Jesus is not a drug, and Christianity cannot guarantee a high at the time or place we may desire it. The criticism which many established Christians directed towards U2 for their song 'I still haven't found what I'm looking for' reflects our unwillingness to admit and face up to our struggles. We need to be honest about the struggles as well as the joys of life as Christians, and ensure that new converts build on the rock of faith rather than on the sands of feelings.

Hope

Hope is an increasingly scarce world resource. On an individual and community level people feel hopeless about their own lives and their futures. It is closely bound up with meaninglessness. 'These are people who to varying degrees make no plans for tomorrow because there are no resources which would make choice a possibility. Today I collect firewood and I shall collect firewood tomorrow.'[7] This Third World hopelessness has its parallels in the way many socially excluded young people in richer nations view life, making no plans for the future: 'Today I shall get stoned and I shall get stoned tomorrow.' Ironically, churches are attracting these young people, not to the services but to their porches and graveyards, quiet places to meet and talk, mess around and hang out. Many spend far more time around church buildings than the church members spend in them. These youngsters arouse feelings of suspicion, fear and guilt. The *Faith in the City* report recognized them:

> There are sizeable groups of young people trapped in Urban Priority Areas who only gain attention when they become a threat, who are denied equality of opportunity and life chances and with whom the churches have little or no contact. It is difficult to exaggerate how alienated these young people are from adult ideas of how young people should behave, from their peers of different social classes and from agencies they think of as acting on adults' behalf, *e.g.* the police, school, the church.[8]

Whatever job schemes or pathways to work may be offered, such young people lack the personal resources or family and community support to break out of this trap. Hope and meaning are things Christians can have in abundance because we believe that Jesus provides a message of hope. It will be our relationship with these young people that shows our concern for them, and our belief in their distinct value and uniqueness as people made in the image of God can be the first drops of moisture on the shrivelled seed of inner hope amid their meaninglessness. Bringing people to faith is an important part of this new hope, but it will almost always arise out of the costly gift of relationship.

Community

Sadly, we must confess that all too often the church does not display signs of community such as the acceptance, unity, love and caring that are found at the rave. Yet, as we have seen, people are desperate for such communion. In many of our activities we gain glimpses of this unity, but they are fleeting and imperfect. The irony is that the one and only thing in which humans are united is sin, yet it is sin which prevents us from experiencing unity and whole relationships with one another and with God. The story that Jesus told about the lost son (Luke 15:11–24) illustrates God's longing for us to return to him, not only so that he can restore us as individuals but so that he can give us a place of significance within his family. For the new life which God gives us is not in isolation from one another but in relationship with one another. We are 'members of God's household' (Ephesians 2:19). This family is the church, God's new community, offering new standards and new relationships.

As such we are faced with a challenge to the quality of our corporate lives as Christians. We need to recognize this with repentance, and seek to recapture the notion and experience of community that were at the heart of the early church (see Acts 2:42–47). And not just the early church: in the Dark Ages, the Celtic church 'modelled a community life that was non-exclusive and deeply attractive to a society that was confused and broken … more than anything else we need a church to model the Spirit-inspired community where people are freed to become fully human. Where this happens, it speaks powerfully to people outside the church.' This means trusting one another, engaging in honest communication without our protective masks, committing ourselves to one another and sharing our joys, sorrows and concerns.

If the church displays this community, it will be powerfully attractive to those who are searching for something missing in their lives, and will make the evangelistic task that much easier.

twelve

where next?

> 'Cheshire Puss,' she began, rather timidly, as
> she did not know whether it would like the
> name: however, it only grinned a little wider.
>   'Would you tell me please, which way I ought to
> go from here?'
>   'That depends a good deal on where you want
> to get to,' said the Cat.

Like the walrus and the carpenter, we have talked of many
things: of the prevalence, patterns and effects of substance
use and the reasons for it, what the Bible says and what a
Christian perspective might be. But we are called to be a
servant people, not just a talking-shop. Actions speak louder
than words, and our talk is no more than a mildly interesting
intellectual exercise if it does not encourage us to change
what we think and what we do. Such change may be
personal, reflected in our own attitudes and our own use of
alcohol and drugs. It may, however, extend beyond ourselves
to have an impact on others, on our local communities and
even our nation. The following are some ways in which
individuals or a church can move in a new direction to make
such contributions.

Thirteen ways to make a difference

1. Get informed

It is important to learn the facts about drugs rather than accepting myths and stereotypes. Reading this book may be the first step. Read other books and leaflets to broaden your perspective, ensuring that you read secular information too, such as (in the UK) the range of Health Education Authority leaflets. Radio programmes and television documentaries on the theme can be enlightening, and an increasing number of films and novels pose the questions for which many people today are seeking answers. Films such as *Drugstore Cowboy*, *Trainspotting* and *Nil by Mouth* may not always be comfortable viewing, but they challenge us to wrestle with important issues. Television and newspaper coverage often errs on the side of sensationalism and needs to be treated with some caution, ideally balanced by some of the more reliable sources of information about drugs and alcohol.

One of the best ways to get informed is to undertake some drug awareness training, perhaps even as a group within a church. Such training is increasingly widely available and is usually delivered in an enjoyable, interesting and relaxed way, over the course of an afternoon or evening. Sessions generally provide information about drug names and effects, and look at our attitudes and use of different drugs. They are suitable for adults of all ages.

2. Parents, keep communicating

Parents are already involved whether they like it or not, because drugs are a fact of life for young people growing up today. Fear that their children might use drugs can be a big problem for some parents, but denial, ignoring the problem or hoping for the best does not make it go away. It is much better to accept that drug availability, like sex, is a reality for young people, and therefore it is important to address it, either directly or indirectly. Reassuringly, this does not require a whole new expertise, since the parenting skills involved in all other aspects of bringing up a child are just as important when it comes to substance use.

There are a number of specific things that you can do as a parent if you become anxious about your child and substances.

First, *get informed* as an important means of increasing your knowledge and enabling you to differentiate between fact and myth. In an increasing number of places, parents' short drug awareness sessions are now available. As well as increasing your confidence, the process of getting informed can be a good way of broaching the subject of drugs and alcohol with children and young people.

Secondly, *maintain good communication* with your children wherever possible. Don't think that because they may know more than you about drugs, particularly illegal ones, it is something you cannot talk about. Avoid lecturing them (hard as this may sometimes seem), and remember that communication is a two-way process – listen to what they have to say as well as telling them what you think and are concerned about. Asking young people what they think about drugs and alcohol is always a useful starting-point, since they will almost certainly have an opinion. If it is still difficult to get started, stories in television programmes, on the news, in the papers or in their own magazines can sometimes provide a good lead-in. Alternatively, get hold of some secular or Christian leaflets and information about drugs and alcohol that are aimed at young people, and ask your children what they think of them. Although it is not always widely publicized, schools in the UK are encouraged to have a drug policy, and drug education is included within the national learning curriculum from an early age. Talk to your children about what they are doing at school, and again, ask them what they or their friends think about drugs and alcohol.

Thirdly, *set an example* in your own use of drugs. Young people are uncannily good at detecting inconsistencies and hypocrisy, and will not only notice your behaviour but may learn from it. Think about your own use of legal and illegal substances as well as prescribed and over-the-counter medicines. Why have you used these things in the past? Why do you use them now? What are your attitudes towards each of them? What do you think is acceptable, at what age or under which circumstances?

Fourthly, *anticipate* how you might react if your children were to come in drunk, if you discovered that they had been smoking or if you thought that they had been trying other substances. As well as thinking about how you might react, consider how you think parents should react and how they should not react.

If you think or know that your children are using alcohol or drugs, try to discuss it with them. Much will depend upon their age and what they are using. Tell them how you feel, but be sure to listen to what they have to say. If this does not achieve anything and you are still worried, seek help and advice – for yourself as much as for them. Don't try to force them to see someone if they don't wish to go. Contact a telephone helpline, an organization such as Adfam, or talk to a friend or someone you can trust. If you go to your doctor for help, avoid getting into the dangerous trap of dealing with the stress you will be feeling by taking pills such as tranquillizers. If your doctor hasn't got time to talk, he or she may not be the right person for you. Above all:

- Don't over-react.
- Don't conduct a major inquisition in the hope of a solution.
- Don't stop communicating with your children.
- Don't stop trying to show your love for your children, whatever sanctions or controls you may decide to put in place.

There are a number of books and sources of advice for parents about general parenting issues and specific concerns about drugs and alcohol.[1]

3. Support an agency

The majority of drug and alcohol services in the UK are

provided by charitable organizations. You or your church may wish to support one by giving or by prayer. Many of the Christian organizations, such as Teen Challenge or the Coke Hole Trust, produce regular prayer guides and newsletters. You may prefer to support more general Christian organizations which help with substance-misuse problems as part of a broader provision of care or outreach. Langley House Trust, Stepping Stones and The 25 Trust are examples of such work. The Evangelical Coalition on Drugs, part of the Evangelical Alliance, can provide contact addresses for most Christian organizations, while the Standing Conference on Drug Abuse (SCODA), the Scottish Drug Forum, Alcohol Concern and the Scottish Council on Alcohol will provide information about relevant local agencies. A list of useful addresses can be found at the end of this book.

4. Provide premises as a resource

It may be that your church has premises that could be used by others. Groups such as Alcoholics Anonymous or Narcotics Anonymous are often in need of cheap or free rooms in which to hold meetings. Over the years these programmes have helped thousands of people, and, though not specifically Christian, they do offer a spiritual route to recovery and for many people are the start of a spiritual awakening. The willingness of a church to offer its premises to any worthwhile external groups can be a positive way to become involved.

5. Pray

Whatever our limitations and restrictions may be, we can always pray. This is not second best, but a vital activity, for if substance misuse is a spiritual problem, there will certainly be spiritual barriers. Prayers can be offered for a variety of situations and needs.

First, we can pray for those using and misusing drugs and alcohol. 'Pray-ers are needed to lend them their faith, hope and confidence in God's freeing and enabling power; to affirm God's will and purpose for their wholeness; to be a channel of positive values and forces of good to combat those of destruction and escape.'[2]

Secondly, those affected by another person's use of alcohol and drugs need our prayers. Alcohol has long been a source of misery, pain and violence for the partners and children of problem drinkers. It is little wonder that children brought up in such homes often grow up to have a range of problems themselves. There is increasing concern too about parents who misuse drugs and the effects of this on their ability to care for their babies and children. Also, there are thousands of parents beside themselves with worry about their children's use of drugs. These people need prayer for protection, strength and deliverance.

Thirdly, those who work within the field of substance misuse need prayer for protection, patience, love, hope and faithfulness. Organizations and individual workers need prayers that 'steadily uphold them in the light and love and redeeming power of God'.[3]

Finally, we can pray for the response of the church and of Christians to the problems and causes of substance misuse.

6. Do voluntary work

There are an increasing number of opportunities for individuals to volunteer their time and skills to help those in need. Most local voluntary-organization councils run a bureau with a register of work. Opportunities for direct work with individuals will vary according to local provision, but can include mentoring programmes, which are an increasingly popular and successful method of providing adult support and friendship for needy young people. Many social-services departments are looking for adults who will act as 'uncles' and 'aunts' to teenagers and children in need. For more information, contact your local social-services or social-work department to check if such a scheme operates in your area. A few counselling agencies seek volunteer counsellors whom they will train and support. Selection and training may be quite rigorous. Contact your local drug agency or your local Council for Voluntary Service to see what is possible in your area.

In all of these areas of work there will be rules and boundaries that must be observed in order to protect all parties involved. These rules may well include restrictions on directly promoting religious views. Although few would prevent you telling someone that you are a Christian, there are likely to be limits on how much direct evangelism is acceptable or appropriate. It is important that any such rules are recognized and honoured. If you feel uncomfortable with them, perhaps that particular helping option is not the right one for you.

7. Develop a service

Maybe there is scope for your local church to establish a ministry relating to drug and alcohol misuse. It is likely that the local need will already be apparent to your church: perhaps it is situated in an area of high drug use, where a number of drug-related deaths and funerals have opened doors of opportunity. Perhaps a number of worried individuals, parents or friends have sought help and support from the church. In thinking about starting such work, never lose sight of the fact that we need to deal with people as total individuals and not define them by their particular problems. Will a service that is specifically about drugs or alcohol exclude others in need?

Before setting up any service, whether voluntary or funded, consult with other local services, particularly the local Drug Action Team co-ordinator. This person can usually be located through the local Health Authority. Talk to others working in the area; partnerships and working together with other agencies are important watchwords for the provision of good services, and it appears high-handed and arrogant if groups, especially churches, seek to go it alone. Don't be put off by negative responses or cynicism about what the church can do, but do try to listen to any comments with as objective a mind as possible, since others may see difficulties, dilemmas or considerations that you have missed.

Local churches in the UK are involved in a widening range of helping activities. First, there are support groups for parents, relatives and friends. There are no simple solutions for those close to someone with a drug or alcohol problem. Support groups offer a safe place for people to talk and gain mutual understanding and help. If you already know of people who would find this helpful, Adfam can offer help and advice in starting such a group (address on p. 162).

Secondly, there are self-help and support groups. These could be for people using tranquillizers or other prescribed medicines, smokers who are seeking to stop, or any other group. Mutual support is the key, but guest speakers can be arranged occasionally to keep the content fresh. The chief factor in all support is that we are meeting people at their point of need. It is likely that, as a result, some of those using such support will look further into what the church is offering without there being any need to offer direct Christian input. Showing care and concern is the biggest expression of Christian love; at times we can spoil it by saying too much too soon.

Finally, telephone helplines, drop-ins, outreach work, befriending schemes and counselling services have all been set up by churches as a response to unmet need in their area. All of these options need very careful planning. Services that start small, evolving and growing over time rather than beginning as some grand design, are more likely to succeed and meet a genuine need.

8. Work for justice

We cannot view drugs and alcohol in isolation from the economic and social structures which shape their use and misuse. Individual Christians and the church as a whole need to be questioning some of the vested interests that benefit from drug and alcohol dependency, and challenging the structural inequalities that give rise to them. This could be done at several levels.

First, *internationally*. Kenneth Leech points to the need for national church groups to consider the international aspects of drug trafficking and trade, including governmental involvement and policies.[4] Global drug trading is a complex matter, full of speculation and anecdotal evidence regarding the involvement of reputable organizations and some security forces. As one leading observer concluded, 'one is tempted to say in the best *X-Files* manner, trust no-one.'[5] We need to hold our own leaders more accountable for the international aspects of the drug trade, rather than simply blaming other countries.

We may also seek to put pressure on the government regarding overseas aid to producer areas. The campaign to reduce Third World debt can only be of benefit in this. Specific support for projects providing viable alternative crops for the Third World peasants who grow opium poppies, cannabis plants or coca bushes can also be a positive way for individuals or churches to get involved. Traidcraft Exchange, Tearfund or Christian Aid can provide information about work that they may be doing in these areas. We also need to show a good deal more compassion and understanding for the helpless drug couriers of South America or Africa, usually women who have been forced into carrying drugs by threats or through poverty, running great risks with little or no remuneration. Those who are caught in Britain invariably serve maximum terms of imprisonment, often without remission and with little or no contact with relatives and children back home. In contrast, the few cases of British women arrested in the Far East for carrying drugs elicit much sympathy and demands for their repatriation; they were 'misguided' or 'victims of a miscarriage of justice', it is claimed. It is no coincidence that the supposedly 'guilty' overseas women in British prisons are almost all black or Asian, whereas the 'innocent' British women in foreign jails are white. Racism is yet one more layer of injustice to be challenged.

Secondly, we can take action *nationally*. This may involve pressing the government about a range of domestic issues, such as legislation, provision of services or education. For example, the 1996 Methodist Conference debated a motion regarding designer drinks and voted to make representations to the government to impose mandatory controls over advertising and availability. We may also be concerned about the state-sponsored dependencies on Valium, Prozac and methadone which have generated millions of pounds for pharmaceutical companies and countless victims in the process.

Finally, we can act *locally*. The easy availability of alcohol and tobacco to young people in public houses and off-licences suggests that pressure is needed to ensure that licensing laws are enforced more effectively. The same goes for the sale of cigarettes to those under sixteen years of age. Lack of activities for young people and under-resourced youth work and community education services are other areas of concern.

National churches, local churches and individuals may make different responses to these problems, and we need to consider carefully how we can go about addressing specific areas, but they are political issues which the church and individual Christians should not shy away from.

9. Offer spiritual leadership and a meaningful spirituality

'Clergy are often seen as leaders, counsellors, social workers and managers but not as spiritual guides,' writes Kenneth Leech. 'It is guidance in the spiritual quest which so many young people want.'[6] Whether this arises out of an attempt by some clergy to find an identity that feels more comfortable in a secular society, or out of a desire by local churches for their ministers to be Jacks of all trades, is unclear. Certainly, however, there is a strong need to allow priests, clergy and ministers the freedom and support to recapture their role of spiritual guides so that they can make the most of the unique opportunities they have to talk about the spiritual life. Ongoing work should not, of course, be left solely to them. There is scope for all Christians to be involved. Such involvement will, says Peter Selby, 'demand of us the most radical understanding of what our religious tradition actually offers the world'.[7]

Even if many people do not overtly recognize the spiritual dimension to their drug use and the questions they are asking, the need for answers is urgent. A youth worker expressed her inability to deal with such issues following the drug-related death of a young woman. Her friends wanted the youth worker to tell them what happened after death and where their friend had gone. She felt unable to help them. Churches, clergy and individual Christians need to place themselves where these sorts of opportunity arise. If we do not, others will do so and may well point them away from the truth.

Tapping into the existing spiritual hunger is not sufficient. Local churches and individual Christians must offer those outside the church a meaningful spirituality. We need to be very clear what we believe and how to communicate this to those we meet, particularly those who do not understand the jargon or 'churchspeak' with which we have become familiar.

Experimentation with forms of worship and services that are intelligible to those who are not used to church (the majority of the population) or who do not feel comfortable in traditional services is essential. Adele Blakebrough of the Kaleidoscope Project identifies the importance of this and the sensitivity that is required. 'I move in this world where people are not used to church language, ideas and background, but they are incredibly interested, endlessly fascinated. They want a voice that draws them in, rather than saying, "These are hurdles you've got to jump before you can be acceptable to us." '[8] Services that touch on people's needs are often a good starting-point. Remembrance services, healing services and young peoples' multimedia worship services can all provide fruitful opportunities. These may be best achieved by working ecumenically, but, whatever the context, they will almost certainly require the slaying of some sacred cows (or at least a co-existence in the same pasture-land). Throughout, we must constantly take our bearings, remembering that we are called to serve others and to feed the hungry hearts.[9]

We also need to recapture and hold on to threads from the cord of Christian tradition that may have been set aside. Over the course of many years, Kenneth Leech has repeatedly emphasized the need to rediscover 'the contemplative and mystical tradition in Christian spirituality and recover a viable pattern of spiritual direction'.[10] The recent resurgence of interest in Celtic spirituality offers us an example of one strand of this diverse Christian tradition, a treasure of great worth that has lain buried.

10. Be a prison or hospital visitor

Many individuals who experience serious drug and alcohol problems end up in prison or in hospital. There may be opportunities to visit individuals in these institutions, usually under the auspices of the respective chaplaincy and with their guidance. Contact the respective chaplains for information. Most prisons have a Prison Fellowship group attached to them. They run prayer groups, Bible study groups for prisoners and befriending services. They offer excellent volunteer training for those who get involved. Prison Fellowship central office (see p. 164) can provide information and a contact number. If you do get involved with hospital or prison work, it is essential that you show respect for the staff who work there, the rules of the organization and boundaries on conduct and faith. Always treat those in hospital or prison as whole individuals rather than labels; they are people, not drug problems, overdoses, drinkers, patients or prisoners.

11. Engage with young people

While it is important that we reach out to individuals from all age groups, young people should be a particular concern. The fifteen- to twenty-five-year-old age group is the one most likely to become involved in drug and alcohol use, and therefore at greatest risk of developing problems. They are at one of the most formative stages of their lives, marking the transition from semi-dependent child to independent adult. They are either under-represented or non-existent within the majority of local churches. Many never come to church, and a significant proportion of those who do come end up leaving because they see it as culturally irrelevant and personally unsatisfying. The problems and issues involved in reaching out and engaging with young people are far beyond the scope of this book, but elsewhere there are some excellent and challenging suggestions about the way forward.[11]

As has already been mentioned, it is particularly ironic that although the established churches cannot attract young people into their buildings when they are open, many cannot get rid of them when the buildings are closed! Hanging out in graveyards and church porches is a popular teenage antidote to boredom. As the *Church Times* reported during the General Synod debate in 1998, even the Dean of Norwich has problems in his cloisters![12] There can be few churches faced with young people hanging around who do not experience an uncomfortable split between members who want to get the police to move the young people on and those who feel that somehow as Christians we ought to be trying to engage with them. Fear is usually the common denominator in these views. Tolerance and acceptance of young people's presence around the church, though not of any associated vandalism and damage, may be a good starting-point. Once more we return to the importance of listening and of trying to build relationships. Understanding young people will certainly make us more tolerant of their situation.

There is also a need for relevant and interesting activities and diversions as an alternative to 'hanging out'. The cuts in local youth services have certainly reduced the options available to young people, and there may be scope for churches to play a part in addressing this problem. The 1996 Methodist Conference identified the need to provide care and attractive alternatives to drugs and alcohol for young people, including non-alcoholic bars and open youth work.[13] Invariably this can be done only as a joint response or as a partnership between church, government and local authorities. Many churches lack the resources or personnel to provide activities, but an open door and a free cup of coffee can convey acceptance and understanding, factors that are so important in establishing relationships with anyone, young people and adults alike.

12. Express community

As we have already seen, drug use and its associated culture have helped to establish a sense of community for many people. Local churches need to look at how they can begin to meet this deep human desire for community. People want to experience a sense of purpose, belonging and personal value, everything that Jesus Christ came to bring and which Christianity should be standing for. It is unlikely that we will draw many people who are searching for community without a much livelier example of Christian fellowship and caring than the legalism, lack of love, self-interest and disunity which exist in many of our churches today.

13. Share the good news

'Biblical social concern is not simply helping casualties on the Jericho Road', writes Kenneth Leech, 'but is the building of a new highway and a new city.'[14] Caring and social action are not enough. John Stott has pointed out that Christians are called to honour both the Great Commandment, 'to love our neighbour' (social action), and the Great Commission, 'to go and make disciples' (evangelism). He helpfully identifies the relationship between social action, and evangelism as one of partnership: 'As partners the two belong to each another and yet are independent of each other. Each stands on its own feet in its own right alongside the other. For each is an end in itself. Both are expressions of unfeigned love.'[15]

Evangelism, then, is not an optional extra but an integral part of Christian mission in the world. All have sinned, and therefore repentance and faith are vital for all. The need for evangelism and conversion is as great for those who have no obvious problems as it is for those who are dependent on drugs or alcohol and whose lives are in chaos as a result. Though the content is the same, the style and approach may vary according to where people are 'coming from', for if they are to understand fully what the Christian faith is about, it needs to be spelt out clearly to them. The ways, shape and form that our evangelism takes will of necessity be varied. The important thing is that, as with the other ways in which we can become involved, evangelism is an integral part of our response to the needs of both individuals and society, giving meaning to life and hope in a world of suffering and despair.

thirteen

dreaming in colour

So she sat on, with closed eyes, and half
believed herself in Wonderland, though she
knew that she had but to open them again and
all would change to dull reality.

Drugs will become an even more important aspect of society in future years. The preoccupation with obtaining pleasure and avoiding pain is already deeply entrenched within our culture. As the demand for chemical 'fix-its' continues to rise, both existing and new substances will be provided by pharmacologists, biochemists, herbalists and other modern-day alchemists, making fortunes from base materials.

Modern society is becoming increasingly like Aldous Huxley's *Brave New World*, as Mark Stibbe has discussed with great insight.[1] Huxley was prophetic, precisely because he was aware of the power and lure of substances and of human beings' desire to experience pleasure and avoid pain. Revisiting his classic novel nearly thirty years later, Huxley observed the increasing importance of mood-altering drugs in society and the similarity of this with the use of 'soma' in his brave new world. Drugs make life that little bit more bearable, though never fully satisfying: 'A hundred doses of happiness are not enough: send to the drug store for another bottle – and when that is finished for another ... There can be no doubt that if tranquillizers could be bought as easily and cheaply as aspirins, they would be consumed, not by the millions as they are at present but by the scores and hundreds of billions. And a good cheap stimulant would be almost as popular.'[2] Today, as Malcolm Muggeridge pointed out, the song remains the same: 'I will lift up my eyes to the pills. Almost everyone takes them, from the humble aspirin to the multi-coloured, king-sized, triple-deckers, which put you to sleep, wake you up, stimulate and soothe you all in one. It is an age of pills.'[3] Bruised and battered in a society scarred by divorce, abuse, violence, fear and hopelessness, individuals turn in on themselves and seek solace in pleasant drug feelings. Here the private drug worlds inside their mind become as real and significant to them as any external reality.

But is this chemical liberation or chemical control? This question is often answered by distinguishing between those whose use of substances dominates their lives because they have become dependent on them, and those who still manage to live 'normal' lives, retaining jobs, homes and relationships without obvious adverse consequences. The former are seen as being chemically controlled, while the latter are somehow regarded as being liberated, because the substance brings all the benefits yet remains under the users' control. From a Christian point of view, they are both chemical control, and any difference is simply a matter of degree. Essentially, they are buying into the same deal in which they depend upon a particular substance to get the desired effect. 'Whatever peace of mind or happiness drugs bring is a packaged peace of mind. When you buy a pill and buy peace with it you get conditioned to cheap solutions instead of deep ones.'[4] In the *Arabian Nights*, there is a tale of beggars who were treated to a 'feast' at which they were given empty plates holding imaginary sumptuous food. However real this feast was in the imagination, the recipients remained hungry and lacked nourishment at the end of it.

Pain and gain

Ultimately the problem is not about drugs. It is about a society which encourages any dependency, be it drugs, sex, work or religion – anything that relieves our pain and struggle and fills the vacuum inside. And it is about human nature and sin. Christianity offers a complete culture shift. It directs us away from a culture that offers quick fixes and easy answers to one where there is doubt, uncertainty and suffering. This is so far at odds with our dominant cultural view that it seems to smack of a masochistic obsession with suffering and pain. Yet this is not a manifesto for self-flagellation – there is quite enough pain to go round without producing more. It is part of the topsy-turvy world of the kingdom where loss is really gain, giving is really receiving and suffering becomes redemptive. Pain and struggle are at the heart of the human condition. Though some endure great suffering and privation compared with others, none of us can avoid it completely. And the testimony of those who have experienced terrible suffering is that somehow God is right there in the middle of it.

In one of Susan Howatch's Starbridge novels, Harriet, a non-believing sculptor, explains the mystery of the relation-ship between creators and their creations. 'No matter how much the mess and distortion make you want to despair, you can't abandon the work ... it's absolutely woven into your soul and you know you can never rest until you've brought truth out of the distortion and beauty out of all the mess. You love the work and you suffer with it and always – always – you're slaving away against all the odds to make everything come right.'[5] Sheila Cassidy has reached a similar conclusion as a result of her experiences of arrest and torture in Chile through to her subsequent hospice work: 'I believe that God has the whole world in his hands. He is not a bystander at the pain of the world ... His are the veins burned by heroin, his the lungs choked by Aids, his is the heart broken by suffering.'[6]

The world that drugs and other more acceptable surrogates shelter us from is messy and painful. There are no simple, easy answers that help us to make sense of the mess; life is full of mystery. Why did Kerry overdose? Why was Debbie abused as a child? Why did Mattie's parents not love him? Why was it that Joe rather than Phil was brought up in poverty? Why did Kathy become HIV positive? We cannot truly know the answers to these questions and the thousands of others that each of us asks; we simply live in the hope and faith that these things are not meaningless. As Sheila Cassidy concludes, 'we will become unstuck if we search for facile explanations of the mystery of suffering instead of bowing down in baffled awe before the one, holy, unknowable God'.[7]

I believe in the Promised Land

Living with this tension does not stop us dreaming of the Promised Land and believing that one day all will be well. This is not about escaping the present, but looking to an assured future. The prophets of old had wonderful dreams and visions about the future. The valleys and mountains would drip with new wine and oil, weapons of war would become tools for peaceful cultivation, the wolf and the lamb would live in peace and the enmity between humankind and God would be at an end. The story of Eden is one to encourage us, since the account of Genesis 1 may also be viewed as an expression of God's plan and purpose in creating. 'Understood in this way,' writes John Sachs, 'what we have is not so much a report about what the world looked like at the beginning, but what it will look like at the end as a result of God's action.'[8] We cannot get back to the Garden, but we can go forward to the future, confident in God's purpose and dream for his world of shalom. His redemptive plan for the world will bring about this peace and wholeness.

Yet the Redeemer, the one who the prophet Isaiah foretold would be the 'Wonderful Counsellor, Mighty God, Everlasting Father, Prince of Peace' (Isaiah 9:6), was also that same prophet's suffering servant who willingly took on himself the sins of the people (Isaiah 53). In following Christ we are also called to be servants and to lose our lives, remembering that Good Friday people become the people of Easter Day. This hope is summed up in the words of Julian of Norwich: 'all shall be well and all shall be well and all manner of thing shall be well'.[9]

As Christians, we must continue to dream in colour. We

dream about how our present lives and service might contribute to the shalom of God's purpose, and we have seen many ways in which this might be done to help those involved with drugs and alcohol. We also dream about our future as the people of God. At the close of *Alice in Wonderland*, Lewis Carroll writes an Easter letter to his readers. He too dreams in colour:

> You will one day see a brighter dawn than this – when lovelier sights will meet your eyes than any waving trees or rippling waters ... and when all the sadness, and the sin, that darkened life on this little earth, shall be forgotten like the dreams of a night that is past!

notes

introduction

1. *Measures for Measures: A Framework for Alcohol Policy* (Alcohol Concern, 1997), p. 3.
2. *idea* magazine (January–March 1998), p. 28.
3. John Stott, *Issues Facing Christians Today* (Marshalls, 1984), p. xi.
4. John Stott, *The Contemporary Christian* (IVP, 1992), pp. 24–29.

one: a world of drugs

1. Chinese legend also attributes the discovery of tea to a Buddhist monk who vowed never to fall asleep so that he might constantly be in communion with God. Needless to say, he did fall asleep, and, on awakening in frustration at his weakness, ripped off his eyelids. Next day he noticed that they had grown roots and a tea plant had grown. He took off two leaves and laid them on his eyes, whereupon two new eyelids grew. He took two more leaves, chewed them and found that they made him feel energized and enabled him to stay awake.

2. P. Mayhew *et al.*, *The 1996 British Crime Survey* (HMSO, 1996).
3. J. Balding, *Young People and Illegal Drugs in 1998* (University of Exeter, 1998).
4. Mayhew *et al.*, *The 1996 British Crime Survey*.
5. A unit of alcohol is equivalent to approximately half a pint of beer, a glass of wine or a single measure of spirits.
6. Office for National Statistics, *Living in Britain: The 1996 General Household Survey* (The Stationery Office, 1998).
7. Harry Shapiro, *Drug Deaths*: Fact Sheet 19. *Druglink* 11.5 (September–October 1996).
8. Shapiro, *Drug Deaths*.
9. Department of Health, *On the State of Public Health 1996* (The Stationery Office, 1997).
10. Kenneth Leech, Drugs and Pastoral Care (Darton, Longman and Todd, 1998), p. 25.
11. Michael Gossop, *Living with Drugs* (Ashgate Publishing, 1998), p. 57.
12. Substance Abuse and Mental Health Services Administration, *National Household Survey on Drug Abuse 1996* (US Government, 1996).
13. *Alcohol Concern* 13.1 (Spring 1998), p. 14.

two: the name of the game

1. The names, packaging, colours and flavours of these drinks were undeniably appealing to young people. Thickhead, a tangerine-flavoured drink with the consistency of half-set jelly, Splooch, a home-brew kit, Supermilch, an alcoholic milk drink, and Spiked Ice, a frozen raspberry vodka mix, made alcoholic lemonades, the first alcopops, look tame. Other names have included Ravers, Love Bytes, TNT Liquid Dynamite, Purple Passion and Dog's Bollocks.
2. Howard Parker, Catherine Bury and Roy Eggington, *New Heroin Outbreaks among Young People in England & Wales* (Police Research Group: Crime Detection and Prevention series, Paper 92, 1998).

3. For example, in the 1980s, when the USSR was breaking up, the face of President Gorbachev featured on a great many tabs of LSD, colloquially known as Gorbies. Similarly, pictures of Saddam Hussein featured during the Gulf War, and more recently pictures of Teletubbies have become common, as the TV programme achieved massive popularity. The use of these and other fun pictures (such as Batman and smily faces) often causes concern that these drugs are targeted at young children. There is no evidence of this, and it seems fairer to say that they aim to convey a sense of fun and humour rather than any deeply sinister intent.

4. World Health Organization, 'Drug Dependence: Its Significance and Characteristics', *WHO Bulletin* 32 (1965), p. 721.

5. Michael Gossop, *Living with Drugs* (Ashgate Publishing, 1998), p. 2.

6. See, for example, Factsheet 13, in *Druglink* 10.3 (May–June 1995); Health Advisory Service, *Children and Young People: Substance Misuse Services* (HMSO, 1996), p. 7.

7. Gossop, *Living with Drugs*, pp. 111–112.

three: drugs and their effects

1. There are periodically instances where heroin users overdose, not because of what has been used to cut and bulk out the heroin, as is sometimes thought, but simply because the drug has not been cut as much as usual and is therefore exceptionally pure. See, for example, Clive Brind *et al.*, 'Solved by the Grapevine', *Druglink* 8.3 (July–August 1993), p. 12, which documents a sudden six-fold increase in heroin overdoses in Brighton among 'people who had been around smack for a long time and knew what they were doing'. It transpired that the normal purity of heroin in Brighton was 20%–35%, while those who had overdosed had been taking heroin of 75% purity. To make matters worse, the £10 bags had contained four times the normal 100mg quantity, so

users were taking larger amounts too.

2. In one experiment carried out at the University of Stockholm, subjects were split into three groups. In one group, people were given a sleeping tablet and told what it was; in another they were given the same tablet and told that the researchers did not know the effect it would have, while in a third group people were given a dummy tablet but told it would make them sleepy. Although the first group showed the greatest response to the drug, there was no difference between those in the other two groups. Other studies have produced similar outcomes. What we expect to happen when we take a drug is therefore very important in determining what actually does happen.

3. 'The Effects of E on Harm Reduction', *Druglink* 11.1 (January–February 1996), p. 4.

4. Michael Gossop, *Living with Drugs* (Ashgate Publishing, 1998), p. 57.

5. Andrew Tyler, *Street Drugs* (Coronet, revised edition, 1995), p. 237.

6. Tyler, *Street Drugs*, p. 162.

7. See, for example, Michael Schofield, *The Strange Case of Pot* (Pelican, 1971), p. 64.

8. An abbreviation of tetrahydrocannabinol.

9. 'Dead Time', *Druglink* 13.5 (September–October 1998), p. 6.

10. There are many sources of information about drug history, effects and risks. The Health Education Council, the Institute for the Study of Drug Dependence and many local drug and alcohol agencies provide useful leaflets giving details about the effects of substances and how to identify them.

four: the reasons

1. Statistics bear out the fact that the illicit use of prescribed drugs such as Valium, temazepam and DF118s is far more widespread in areas of high unemployment such as Scotland and northeast England.

2. Nicholas Dorn and Karim Murji, *Drug Prevention: A Review of the English Language Literature* (Institute for the Study of Drug Dependence, 1992), pp. 7–12.
3. Melvin Burgess, *Junk* (Penguin, 1997), p. 144.
4. Thomas De Quincy, *Confessions of an English Opium Eater* (1821; Henry Frowde, London, 1903), p. 189.
5. See Michael Gossop, *Living with Drugs* (Ashgate Publishing, 1998), pp. 148–151, for a useful discussion about crack, the media and the drug's alleged addictiveness.
6. Nicholas Saunders, *Ecstasy and the Dance Culture* (Nicholas Saunders, 1995), p. 224.
7. Howard S. Becker, *Outsiders* (Free Press, New York, 1963), p. 53.
8. In Fiona Measham, Howard Parker and Judith Aldridge, *Starting, Switching, Slowing and Stopping* (Home Office, 1998), p. 17.
9. In Measham *etc.*, *Starting, Switching*, p. 21.
10. At the time of writing, there is much talk on the streets of the potential of Viagra when taken with amphetamine. Viagra alone is likely to have black-market potential, and the police anticipate an increase in pharmacy burglaries as a result.
11. Sheila Henderson, *Ecstasy: Case Unsolved* (Pandora, 1997), pp. 67–73, 91–96.
12. C. J. Stone, *Fierce Dancing* (Faber and Faber, 1996), pp. 232, 233.
13. Sir Arthur Conan Doyle, *The Complete Sherlock Holmes* (Penguin, 1981), p. 89.
14. William Burroughs, *Junky* (Penguin, 1977), p. 125.

five: in the beginning

1. In the Canadian Government Commission of Inquiry, *The Non-Medical Use of Drugs* (Penguin, 1971), p. 389.
2. Andrew Tyler, *Street Drugs* (Coronet, revised edition, 1995), p. 247.
3. Quoted in Harry Shapiro, *Waiting for the Man* (Mandarin, 1990), p. 197.

4. In *Viz* magazine. *Viz* is a bi-monthly humorous comic with a readership of more than 1 million. Although it should be sold only to over eighteens, *Viz* is cult reading for many teenage boys from thirteen years of age upwards.

5. These 'new' drugs are almost always previously known substances marketed as something new. Herbal Ecstasy, for example, is often a drug called ephedra, from which the prescription drug ephedrine (also used in cold remedies) is extracted. Ephedra and ephedrine are stimulant drugs.

6. www.phat.demon.uk/herbal_crack.html.

7. Quoted in Nicholas Saunders, *Ecstasy and the Dance Culture* (Nicholas Saunders, 1995), p. 159.

8. Thomas Szasz, *Ceremonial Chemistry* (Routledge and Kegan Paul, 1975), pp. 63–64.

9. Morphine is around ten times more powerful than opium, while heroin in turn is nearly four times stronger than morphine.

10. See Michael Gossop, *Living With Drugs* (Ashgate Publishing, 1998), pp. 172–174. One of the abiding ironies of the current UK problem in preventing incoming supplies of heroin from the Far East is the fact that Britain benefited from first developing and subsequently supplying an enormous market for opium in China despite the Emperor's appeals to Queen Victoria to stop the trade. The consequences of the subsequent Opium War are still with us today.

11. C. S. Lewis, *The Problem of Pain* (1957; Fount, 1977), p. 72.

12. Commission on Social and Bio-ethical Questions of the Lutheran Church of Australia, *Social Statement on the Use of Drugs* (Lutheran Church of Australia, 1979), paragraph 6.

13. Commission on Social and Bio-ethical Questions of the Lutheran Church of Australia, *Social Statement on the Use of Drugs*, paragraph 6.

14. Paul Tournier, *A Doctor's Casebook in the Light of the Bible* (Highland, 1983), p. 54.

15. Richard Holloway, *Signs of Glory* (Darton, Longman and Todd, 1982), p. 45.
16. Quoted in John Smith, 'Maybe Your Mother Would Like it After All', *Third Way* 17.9 (November 1994), p. 35.

six: specific bible principles: alcohol

1. 'News', *Druglink* 11.6 (November–December 1996), p. 4.
2. See Dave Cave, *A Biblical Theology of Addiction* (Evangelical Coalition on Drugs, 1993). I am particularly indebted to this booklet, which helped to lay the foundations for this chapter.
3. The fact that there are a number of names differentiating various forms of wine indicates the important part that it played in society. In contrast, during Old Testament times, the Israelites were not much involved in the fishing trade, and there is only one Hebrew word for 'fish', covering everything from a tiddler to the great fish that swallowed Jonah. In later New Testament times, fishing on Galilee had developed, as had the names for different fish.
4. Water drawn from wells was generally safe enough to use for cooking, but the water collected from the roof was not hygienic, and even with the advent of Roman-built aqueducts the water was still not fit to drink.
5. See Proverbs 23:20, 30–31; Isaiah 5:11–24; Isaiah 28:1–8. V. M. Matthew has written a fascinating article on the symptomatology of excessive drinking described in these passages, arguing that they demonstrate a high level of consistency with our contemporary understanding about the physiological and psychological symptoms of alcohol dependence, such as tolerance, withdrawal symptoms, alcohol-induced hallucinations, memory blackouts and relief drinking. See V. M. Matthew, 'Alcoholism in Biblical Prophecy', *Alcohol & Alcoholism* 27.1 (1992), pp. 88–90.

6. See, for example, Revelation 14:8; 16:19 or 18:3.
7. See, for example, Genesis 14:18; Esther 1:7; Isaiah 25:6.
8. Matthew 26:29; Mark 14:25; Luke 22:18.
9. See, for example, Deuteronomy 7:13; 2 Kings 18:32; Joel 2:19; Amos 9:13.
10. The Independent Order of Rechabites, named after this family, was founded in around the fourteenth century as a society devoted to abstention from alcohol.

seven: general biblical principles

1. James 3:1–12 vividly describes the difficulties we face in controlling what we say. It is much more difficult when we are under the influence of drink or drugs.
2. Quoted in *Drink Talking*, shown on BBC2 in 1992.
3. Social-learning theory suggests that individuals begin to use drugs as a result of observing others using drugs (parents, peers, heroes, celebrities, *etc.*), and engage in a new behaviour because of this. What is already a learned behaviour is then reinforced when they discover the rewards of doing it (pleasure, release, acceptability, status, *etc.*). Individuals therefore engage in drug and alcohol use for pleasure and continue to use them because of the anticipated positive outcomes (pleasure, tension reduction, 'getting a buzz', forgetting bad feelings, gaining energy and confidence, *etc.*).

eight: principles and practicalities

1. Commission on Social and Bio-ethical Questions of the Lutheran Church of Australia, *Social Statement on the Use of Drugs* (Lutheran Church of Australia, 1979), paragraph 3.
2. There is still a considerable amount that we do not know about drug-related harm. For example, controversy still rages about cannabis; some research is very value-laden, and the 'pro' and 'anti' camps make so much of research evidence that supports their positions that it is very hard

to get a clear picture of what physical harm cannabis actually causes.

3. Tolerance occurs when the body adjusts to the effects of the drug, and more is required to get the same feeling. In some drugs such as heroin, alcohol or Ecstasy, tolerance builds up particularly quickly. The person who drinks three glasses of wine every day feels much less intoxicated on this daily dose than would someone who had not had a drink for several months.

4. Henri Nouwen, *Here and Now* (Darton, Longman and Todd, 1994), p. 128.

5. Some people claim that heroin and cocaine addicts become dependent because they are seeking to replicate the first-time experience. Alas, it remains an illusive one hit away.

6. Andy Thornton, 'The Drugs Debate: An Injection of Reality?' *Third Way* 20.1 (February 1997), pp. 9–10.

7. Department of Transport, *The Facts About Drinking and Driving* (Transport and Road Research Laboratory, 1986).

8. Radio Five Live's *Breakfast* show, 26 October 1998.

9. Sister Alison Mary, *Christianity and Addiction* (New Life Press, 1970), p. 267.

10. Alcoholics Anonymous World Services Inc.

nine: inside the gates of eden

1. Paul Tournier, *The Whole Person in a Broken World* (Collins, 1965), p. 8.

2. Nicky Gumbel, *Questions of Life* (Kingsway, 1995), p. 12.

3. Richard Holloway, *Signs of Glory* (Darton, Longman and Todd, 1982), p. 12.

4. In John Dainith and Amanda Isaacs (eds.), *Medical Quotes* (Market House Books, 1989), p. 143.

5. C. J. Stone, *Fierce Dancing* (Faber and Faber, 1996), p. 14.

6. Aldous Huxley, *The Doors of Perception* (1954; Chatto and Windus, 1977), p. 54.

7. In Nicholas Saunders, *Ecstasy and the Dance Culture* (Nicholas Saunders, 1995), p. 41.

8. An interview with *Queen & Life* magazine, quoted in Harry Shapiro, *Waiting for the Man* (Mandarin, 1990), p. 145.

9. Canadian Government Commission of Inquiry, *The Non-Medical Use of Drugs* (Penguin, 1971), p. 386.

10. In Saunders, *Ecstasy and the Dance Culture*, p. 40.

11. In Saunders, *Ecstasy and the Dance Culture*, p. 185.

12. Alun Morinan, 'Letters', *Third Way* 20.1 (February 1997), p. 11.

13. Saunders, *Ecstasy and the Dance Culture*, p. 157.

14. In Sheila Henderson, *Ecstasy: Case Unsolved* (Pandora, 1997), p. 56.

15. Henderson, *Ecstasy: Case Unsolved*, p. 51.

16. Hilary Klee and Paul Reid, *Amphetamine Misusing Groups* (Home Office, 1995), p. 25.

17. Quoted in Steve Turner, *Hungry for Heaven* (Kingsway, 1988), p. 149.

18. Stone, *Fierce Dancing*, p. 22.

19. Richard Holloway, *Signs of Glory* (Darton, Longman and Todd, 1982), p. 45.

20. Saunders, *Ecstasy and the Dance Culture*, pp. 122–123, tells of a Benedictine monk who tried Ecstasy and found that it increased his understanding and ability to pray. He maintained that benefits could come only 'when you are already looking in the right direction. It should not be used unless one is really searching for God.'

21. Henri Nouwen, *Here and Now* (Darton, Longman and Todd, 1994), p. 30.

22. C. S. Lewis, *The Weight of Glory* (SPCK, 1954), p. 8.

ten: wake-up call

1. Gerald Olsen, '"Physician, Heal Thyself": Drink, Temperance and the Medical Question in the Victorian and Edwardian Church of England, 1830–1914', *Addiction* 89 (1994), p. 1170.

2. Maine became the first state to introduce prohibition

in 1846, some seventy-two years before the 18th Amendment to the US Constitution in 1919 prohibited the manufacture, sale and transportation of alcoholic drinks.

3. Virginia Berridge, 'What's Happening in History', *British Journal of Addiction* 81 (1986), p. 722. Olsen, in '"Physician, Heal Thyself": Drink, Temperance and the Medical Question', p. 1172, notes that in 1860, alcohol accounted for over a fifth of the total expenditure at University College Hospital, London. There were, however, dissenting voices. In 1804, Thomas Trotter, an Edinburgh physician, wrote 'An Essay, Medical, Philosophical and Chemical, on Drunkeness and its Effects on the Human Body', in which he identified both physical and mental harm resulting from excessive drinking. Interestingly, some of the information put out by the temperance societies also challenged the accepted medical wisdom. One leaflet declared: 'Alcohol reduces vitality and the power of resisting disease.'

4. Olsen, '"Physician, Heal Thyself": Drink, Temperance and the Medical Question', p. 1169.

5. Olsen, '"Physician, Heal Thyself": Drink, Temperance and the Medical Question', p. 1170.

6. Olsen, '"Physician, Heal Thyself": Drink, Temperance and the Medical Question', p. 1173.

7. The Task Force to Review Services for Drug Misusers, *Independent Review of Drug Treatment Services* (Department of Health, 1996), p. 68.

8. Eric Blakebrough, *No Quick Fix* (Marshall Pickering, 1986).

9. Harm is seen as being on a continuum with abstinence at one end, and chaotic, injecting drug use involving a variety of drugs at the other. The aim of harm reduction or harm minimization is to move people down the scale, though abstinence from drugs is not necessarily the goal. Although at one level it is about provision of care for individuals, it is essentially a public-health initiative because HIV was deemed to be a greater threat to public and individual health than drug misuse. There is

evidence that provisions such as prescribing methadone to heroin users does reduce the crime level, though how far it helps people move towards abstinence is far from clear.

eleven: a shot of love

1. Quoted in Malcolm Muggeridge, *Something Beautiful for God* (Fontana, 1972), pp. 73–74.
2. Bill Kirkpatrick (ed.), *Cry Love, Cry Hope: Responding to AIDS* (Darton, Longman and Todd, 1994).
3. Muggeridge, *Something Beautiful for God*, pp. 73–74.
4. Kenneth Leech, *Drugs and Pastoral Care* (Darton, Longman and Todd, 1998), p. 100.
5. Greenbelt Seminar Tapes 1994, 'Advice from a Tribal Elder: Never Forget your Roots.'
6. Sheila Cassidy, Foreword, in Kirkpatrick (ed.), *Cry Love, Cry Hope*, p. x.
7. Peter Cotterell, *Mission and Meaninglessness* (SPCK, 1990), p. 266.
8. *Faith in the City* (Church House Publishing, 1985), p. 315.
9. Michael Mitton, *Restoring the Woven Cord* (Darton, Longman and Todd, 1995), p. 47.

twelve: where next?

1. See, for example, Martin Herbert, *Living with Teenagers* (Basil Blackwell, 1987), or Julian Cohen and James Kay, *Taking Drugs Seriously* (Thorsons, 1994), for examples of secular books. For examples of a Christian perspective, see Grahame Knox, *Drugs and Young People* (Kingsway, 1989), or Nick Pollard, *Why Do They Do That? Understanding Teenagers* (Lion, 1998) .
2. Sister Alison Mary, *Christianity and Addiction* (New Life Press, 1970), p. 25.
3. Sister Alison Mary, *Christianity and Addiction*, p. 26.
4. Kenneth Leech, *Drugs and Pastoral Care* (Darton, Longman and Todd, 1998), pp. 119–120.

5. Roger Lewis, 'High Times, Low Company', *Druglink* 13.6 (November–December 1998), p. 22.
6. Kenneth Leech, *Youthquake* (Sheldon Press, 1973), p. 198.
7. Peter Selby, *Liberating God* (SPCK, 1983), p. 89.
8. Adele Blakebrough, 'Love in a Different Vein', *Third Way* 20.8 (October 1997), p. 15.
9. For further reading about increasing our spiritual and cultural relevance, see Jack Burton, *The Gap* (Triangle, 1991), and Mike Breen, *Growing the Smaller Church* (Marshall Pickering, 1992),
10. Leech, *Youthquake*, p. 196–197.
11. See *e.g.* Peter Brierley, *Reaching and Keeping Teenagers* (Monarch, 1993); Breen, *Growing the Smaller Church*, pp. 60–74.
12. 'Young People Join Drugs Debate', *Church Times* (10 July 1998), p. 4.
13. Report on the Methodist Conference, 1995.
14. Kenneth Leech, *The Social God* (Sheldon Press, 1981), p. 12.
15. John Stott, *Christian Mission in the Modern World* (Falcon, 1975), p. 27.

thirteen: dreaming in colour

1. Mark Stibbe, *O Brave New Church* (Darton, Longman and Todd, 1995).
2. Aldous Huxley, *Brave New World Revisited* (1959; Flamingo, 1994), pp. 111–112.
3. Malcolm Muggeridge, in the *New Statesman*, 3 August 1992.
4. Max Lehrner, 'The Assault on the Mind', *The Unfinished Country*.
5. Susan Howatch, *Absolute Truths* (HarperCollins, 1995), p. 406.
6. Sheila Cassidy, *Sharing the Darkness* (Darton, Longman and Todd, 1988), pp. 157–158.
7. Cassidy, *Sharing the Darkness*, p. 154.
8. John R. Sachs, 'Spirituality for an Ecological Age', in

Robert J. Wicks (ed.), *Handbook of Spirituality* (Paulist Press, New York, 1995), p. 432.
9. Dame Julian of Norwich, *Revelations of Divine Love*, ch. 27.

glossary of drug terms

Alcoholics Anonymous (AA). The organization was founded in 1935 in the USA. The core of AA is the twelve-step programme which members work through, supported by others recovering from alcohol problems. AA regards alcoholism as a disease.

Alcoholism. A term given to problematic drinking, particularly by AA and twelve-step programmes, implying the absence of volition. They regard alcoholism as a disease. The term 'alcoholism' has largely been replaced by 'problem drinking'.

Benzodiazepines. The collective name for the group of tranquillizers which include Valium, temazepam, Ativan (lorazepam), Rohypnol (flunitrazepam).

Chasing the dragon. A term that usually refers to smoking heroin, because the smoke that rises from the foil looks like the coils of a dragon's tail.

Controlled drugs. Drugs whose manufacture, supply and possession are controlled under the Misuse of Drugs Act

1971. The Misuse of Drugs Regulations 1985 define the classes of people who are authorized to supply and possess controlled drugs while acting in their professional capacity.

Cut. The addition of adulterants to powdered drugs, to increase the quantity prior to being sold. Cutting leads to variable quality, and to possible harm, depending upon the adulterant used.

Delirium tremens (DTs). Physical alcohol withdrawal symptoms: shaking, agitation, restlessness, hallucinations and distortion of time.

Dependency. The state of being physically or psychologically addicted to a substance. The user feels compelled to use it in order to remain physically well or psychologically able to function.

Depressants. Drugs that act on the central nervous system to slow the body down. Alcohol, heroin and Valium are all depressant drugs.

Detoxification. Often referred to as 'detox'. This is the process whereby a dependent drug user is helped to stop by being prescribed reducing amounts of the same or another drug. This helps to avoid physical complications, minimizes the discomfort and reduces the likelihood of early relapse.

Drug. Any chemical substance, whether of natural or synthetic origin, which can be used to alter perception, mood or other psychological state.

Drug abuse. Harmful use of a drug or combination of substances. 'Drug misuse' is the preferred term.

Drug Action Team (DAT), set up by the 1995 White Paper *Tackling Drugs Together*. Teams largely consist of senior members of health services and social services and are usually set up within health-authority or local-authority boundaries.

Drug misuse. The use of a drug, or combination of substances, that is physically and/or psychologically harmful.

Drug Reference Group (DRG). Operational members of key local agencies such as the housing department, social services, GPs, drugs agencies and youth work, who advise and support the work of the DAT at ground level.

Drug use. Usually refers to the consumption of a substance that does not cause any perceptible immediate harm, though it may carry some degree of risk.

Escalation theory. The idea that using one drug automatically leads to the use of other more dangerous substances. In its commonest form it states that smoking cannabis leads to heroin addiction.

Experimental drug use. Trying out or experimenting with a substance, typical of the early stages of an individual's involvement with drugs.

Flashbacks. Hallucinations and drug experiences which happen spontaneously a long time after the drug was used. Most commonly associated with LSD.

Hallucinogens. Drugs which alter perception and induce hallucinations in the user. Sometimes referred to as psychedelics. Examples are LSD and magic mushrooms.

Hard drugs. A popular term often used by the media to refer to more dangerous drugs, as distinct from 'soft drugs' which are viewed as less dangerous. It is not a useful term because it gives the idea that some drugs are much safer than others.

Harm reduction. This approach accepts that people are using substances and that they may well continue to do so, but encourages them to use less harmful substances in less harmful ways.

Maintenance. The prescribing of a substitute drug in order to reduce an individual's use of a particular substance or to reduce the harm caused by the method of administration.

Narcotics Anonymous (NA) operates like Alcoholics Anonymous except that members have drug rather than alcohol problems. There are offshoots such as Cocaine Anonymous.

Opiates. Painkilling drugs derived from the opium poppy, such as opium, morphine and heroin.

Opioids. Generic term for painkilling drugs, both those derived from the opium poppy and those artificially made and similar to opiates in their effect. In addition to the opiates (see above) this term also includes methadone, DF118s, pethadine and temgesic. The two terms are sometimes used interchangeably.

Poly-drug use. Sometimes referred to as 'poly-substance use'. The use of one drug to enhance or counter the effects of another.

Recreational drug use. Drinking or drug-taking as a recreation or a pastime. It often becomes a social activity that is a part of a person's lifestyle.

Relapse. A return to dependent drug use after a period of abstinence or control. Relapse prevention work involves helping individuals to identify triggers and risk situations that might induce relapse, as well as rehearsing how to deal with these.

Script. A prescription. It usually refers to the prescribing of a drug such as methadone, as a substitute for one on which an individual is dependent.

Sedatives. Drugs that slow down the central nervous system, causing drowsiness and sleep.

Soft drugs. A popular term often used by the media to refer to less dangerous drugs, as distinct from 'hard drugs' which are viewed as more dangerous. It is not a useful term because it gives the idea that some drugs are much safer than others.

Stimulants. Drugs that act on the central nervous system to speed the body up and increase mental activity. Examples are cocaine, amphetamine and caffeine.

Substance abuse. See 'Drug abuse'.

Substance misuse. See 'Drug misuse'.

Substance use. See 'Drug use'.

Therapeutic community. A particular approach to treatment, usually residential, in which the individuals, structures and activities are the treatment. Most are hierarchical and involve high levels of confrontation to enable individuals to face up to their dependent behaviour.

Tolerance. The process whereby the body gets used to particular substances and requires ever higher doses to get the same effect.

Turkey. Also called 'cold turkey'. The withdrawal from drugs, usually heroin, marked by shivering, goosebumps, aches, sickness and flu-like symptoms.

Twelve-step programmes. Used in AA and NA programmes and sometimes referred to as the Minnesota model. Drug users admit their powerlessness over their life and substance use, surrender to a 'higher power' and work through the twelve steps.

useful addresses

This is a limited address list intended to give the United Kingdom reader some useful starting-points for following up ideas in the book and obtaining further information.

Policy

UK Anti-Drugs Co-ordination Unit, 59/2, Government Offices, Great George Street, London SW1P 3AL. Tel. 0171 270 5776. (Government Drugs Co-ordination.)

Information

Alcohol Concern, Waterbridge House, 32–36 Loman Street, London SE1 0EE. Tel. 0171 928 7377. (Library, information service, *etc.*, on alcohol.)

Health Education Authority, Trevelyan House, 30 Great Peter Street, London SW1P 2HW. Tel. 0171 222 5300.

The Institute for the Study of Drug Dependence (ISDD), Waterbridge House, 32–36 Loman Street, London SE1 0EE. Tel. 0171 928 1211. (Information about drugs except tobacco and alcohol; publications, library, information, *etc.*)

Re-Solv, 30a High Street, Stone, Staffordshire ST15 8AW. Tel. 01785 817885. (Solvents – directory of help, information, teaching materials, *etc.*)

SCODA (The Standing Conference on Drug Abuse), Waterbridge House, 32–36 Loman Street, London SE1 0EE. Tel. 0171 928 9500. (Practice guidelines, publications, information about local services, *etc.*)

Scottish Council on Alcohol, 2nd Floor, 166 Buchanan Street, Glasgow G1 2NH. Tel. 0141 333 9677.

Scottish Drugs Forum, Shaftesbury House, 5 Waterloo Street, Glasgow G1 5QR. Tel. 0141 221 1175.

Help and support

Adfam, 32–36 Loman Street, London SE1 0EE. Tel. 0171 928 8900. (Support and information for friends and families of drug users.)

Al Anon Family Groups, 61 Great Dover Street, London SE1 4YF. Tel. 0171 403 0888. (For friends and relatives of problem drinkers.)

Alcoholics Anonymous: phone 01904 644026 for details of local groups.

Drinkline: 0345 32 02 02. (Helpline with information and advice about alcohol.)

Drug helplines: England and Wales, 0800 77 66 00; Scotland, 0800 77 68 711. (24-hour information and advice about drugs.)

Narcotics Anonymous: phone 0171 251 4007 for details of local groups.

Education and Training

Tacade, 1 Hulme Place, The Crescent, Salford, Greater Manchester M5 4QA. Tel. 0161 745 8925. (Education and training, resources, consultancy.)

Miscellaneous

National Council of Voluntary Organizations (NCVO), Regent's Wharf, 8 All Saints Street, London N1 9RL. Tel. 0171 713 6161.

Christian Organizations

Christian Aid (UK Head Office), 35 Lower Marsh, London SE1 7RT. Tel. 0171 620 4444.

Church of Scotland Board of Social Responsibility, Charis House, 47 Milton Road East, Edinburgh EH15 2SR. Tel. 0131 657 2000. (Residential rehabilitation, counselling and outreach services.)

Coke Hole Trust, 70 Junction Road, Andover, Hants. SP10 32X. Tel. 01264 361745. (Residential rehabilitation.)

Evangelical Alliance Coalition on Drugs, Evangelical Alliance, Whitefield House, 186 Kennington Park Road, London SE11 4BT. Tel. 0171 207 2150.

Hope UK, 25(f) Copperfield Street, London SE1 0EN. Tel. 0171 928 0840. (Leaflets, education and training.)

Kaleidoscope Project, 40 Cromwell Road, Kingston-upon-Thames KT2 6RE. Tel. 0181 549 2681. (Day centre and prescribing service.)

Langley House Trust, 46 Market Square, Witney, Oxon OX8 6AL. Tel. 01993 774075. (Operates over a dozen hostels and accommodation projects for ex-offenders, including two specialist centres for those with drug and alcohol problems.)

The Matthew Project, 24 Pottersgate, Norwich NR2 1DX. Tel. 01603 626 123. (Help, support, information and advice.)

Prison Fellowship, PO Box 945, Maldon, Essex CM9 4EW. Tel. 01621 843232. (National prison ministry.)

Stepping Stones, PO Box 344, Richmond, Surrey TW9 1GQ. Tel. 0181 287 5524. (Accommodation project.)

Tearfund (UK Head Office), 100 Church Road, Teddington, Middlesex TW11 8QE. Tel. 0181 977 9144.

Teen Challenge UK, 52 Penygroes Road, Gorlas, Llanelli SA14 7LA. Tel. 01269 842718. (Residential rehabilitation and outreach work throughout the UK.)

Traidcraft Exchange, Traidcraft plc, Kingsway, Gateshead, Tyne and Wear NE11 0NE. Tel. 0191 491 0591.

The 25 Trust, PO Box 692, Carshalton, Surrey, SM5 2ZR. (Prison and special hospital ministry, especially in southern England.)

Yeldall Manor, Blakes Lane, Hare Hatch, Reading RG10 9XR. Tel. 0118 940 1093. (Residential rehabilitation.)

bibliography

Sister Alison Mary, *Christianity and Addiction* (New Life Press, 1970).

Howard S. Becker, *Outsiders* (Free Press, New York, 1963).

Virginia Berridge, 'What's Happening in History', *British Journal of Addiction* 81 (1986), pp. 721–723.

Adele Blakebrough, 'Love in a Different Vein', *Third Way* 20.8 (October 1997), p. 15.

Eric Blakebrough, *No Quick Fix* (Marshall Pickering, 1986).

Mike Breen, *Growing the Smaller Church* (Marshall Pickering, 1992).

Peter Brierley, *Reaching and Keeping Teenagers* (Monarch, 1993).

Melvin Burgess, *Junk* (Penguin, 1997).

William Burroughs, *Junky* (Penguin, 1977).

Jack Burton, *The Gap* (Triangle, 1991).

Canadian Government Commission of Inquiry, *The Non-Medical Use of Drugs* (Penguin, 1971).

Lewis Carroll, *Alice's Adventures in Wonderland* (1865; Penguin Classics, 1994).

————, *Through the Looking Glass* (1871; Penguin Classics, 1994).

Sheila Cassidy, *Sharing the Darkness* (Darton, Longman and Todd, 1988).

Dave Cave, *A Biblical Theology of Addiction* (Evangelical Coalition on Drugs, 1993).

Julian Cohen and James Kay, *Taking Drugs Seriously* (Thorsons, 1994).

Commission on Social and Bio-ethical Questions of the Lutheran Church of Australia, *Social Statement on the Use of Drugs* (Lutheran Church of Australia, 1979).

Peter Cotterell, *Mission and Meaninglessness* (SPCK, 1990).

Thomas De Quincy, *Confessions of an English Opium Eater* (1821; Henry Frowde, London, 1903).

Department of Health, *The Task Force to Review Services for Drug Misusers* (Department of Health, 1996).

Francis Dewar, *Live for a Change* (Darton, Longman and Todd, 1988).

Nicholas Dorn and Karim Murji, *Drug Prevention: A Review of the English Language Literature* (Institute for the Study of Drug Dependence, 1992).

Faith in The City (Church House Publishing, 1985).

Michael Gossop, *Living with Drugs* (Ashgate Publishing, 1998).

Nicky Gumbel, *Questions of Life* (Kingsway, 1995).

Health Advisory Service, *Children and Young People: Substance Misuse Services* (HMSO, 1996).

Sheila Henderson, *Ecstasy: Case Unsolved* (Pandora, 1997).

Martin Herbert, *Living with Teenagers* (Basil Blackwell, 1987).

Richard Holloway, *Signs of Glory* (Darton, Longman and Todd, 1982).

Susan Howatch, *Absolute Truths* (HarperCollins, 1995).

Aldous Huxley, *Brave New World Revisited* (1959; Flamingo, 1994).

———— , *The Doors of Perception* (1954; Chatto and Windus, 1977).

Bill Kirkpatrick (ed.), *Cry Love, Cry Hope: Responding to AIDS* (Darton, Longman and Todd, 1994).

Hilary Klee and Paul Reid, *Amphetamine Misusing Groups* (Home Office, 1995).

Grahame Knox, *Drugs and Young People* (Kingsway, 1989).

Kenneth Leech, *Drugs and Pastoral Care* (Darton, Longman and Todd, 1998).

————, *The Social God* (Sheldon Press, 1981).

————, *Youthquake* (Sheldon Press, 1973).

C. S. Lewis, *The Problem of Pain* (1957; Fount, 1977).

————, *The Weight of Glory* (SPCK, 1954).

Roger Lewis, 'High Times, Low Company', *Druglink* 13.6 (November–December 1998).

V. M. Matthew, 'Alcoholism in Biblical Prophecy', *Alcohol & Alcoholism* 27.1 (1992).

Fiona Measham, Howard Parker and Judith Aldridge, *Starting, Switching, Slowing and Stopping* (Home Office, 1998).

Michael Mitton, *Restoring the Woven Cord* (Darton, Longman and Todd, 1995).

Malcolm Muggeridge, *Something Beautiful for God* (Fontana, 1972).

Henri Nouwen, *Here and Now* (Darton, Longman and Todd, 1994).

————, *Seeds of Hope* (Darton, Longman and Todd, 1989).

Gerald Olsen, '"Physician, Heal Thyself": Drink, Temperance and the Medical Question in the Victorian and Edwardian Church of England, 1830–1914', *Addiction* 89 (1994).

Howard Parker, Catherine Bury and Roy Eggington, *New Heroin Outbreaks among Young People in England and Wales* (Police Research Group: Crime Detection and Prevention series, Paper 92, 1998).

Nicholas Saunders, *Ecstasy and the Dance Culture* (Nicholas Saunders, 1995).

Michael Schofield, *The Strange Case of Pot* (Pelican, 1971).

Peter Selby, *Liberating God* (SPCK, 1983).

Harry Shapiro, *Waiting for the Man* (Mandarin, 1990).

John Smith, *Cutting Edge* (Monarch, 1992).

————, 'Maybe Your Mother Would Like it After All' *Third Way* 17.9 (November 1994).

————, 'No Smoke Without Fire' *Third Way* 17.8 (October 1994).

Mark Stibbe, *O Brave New Church* (Darton, Longman and Todd, 1995).

C. J. Stone, *Fierce Dancing* (Faber and Faber, 1996).

John R. W. Stott, *Christian Mission in The Modern World* (Falcon, 1975).

————, *The Contemporary Christian* (IVP, 1992).

————, *Issues Facing Christians Today* (Marshalls, 1984).

————, *Your Mind Matters* (UCCF, 1972).

Thomas Szasz, *Ceremonial Chemistry* (Routledge and Kegan Paul, 1975).

Jamie Thompson and Ollie Batchelor, *Substance Misuse: An Open Learning Pack* (University of Northumbria, 1997).

Andy Thornton, 'The Drugs Debate: An Injection of Reality?' *Third Way* 20.1 (February 1997).

Paul Tournier, *A Doctor's Casebook in the Light of the Bible* (Highland, 1983).

————, *The Whole Person in a Broken World* (Collins, 1965).

Steve Turner, *Hungry for Heaven* (Kingsway, 1988).

Andrew Tyler, *Street Drugs* (Coronet, revised edition, 1995).

Irvine Welsh, *Trainspotting* (Martin Secker and Warburg, 1993).

index

Matters of Life and Death

JOHN WYATT

The dilemmas behind some newspaper headlines concern us all. What medical science *can* do and what it *ought* to do – or ought not to do – impinges upon our personal lives, our families and our society.

In this book, John Wyatt examines issues surrounding the beginning and end of life – fertility treatments, genetics, abortion, infanticide, the dying baby, euthanasia and physician-assisted suicide – against the background of current medical–ethical thought. Writing out of a deep conviction that the Bible's view of our humanness points a way forward, he suggests how Christian healthcare professionals, lay people and churches can respond to the challenges and opportunities that confront us.

'*Many healthcare professionals will want this reasoned, evidenced and challenging account of a range of vital ethical issues in contemporary medicine. But it deserves a wide readership beyond those involved immediately with healthcare, for these issues are truly of public concern.*'

DUNCAN VERE
Professor Emeritus of Therapeutics, University of London

'*Professor Wyatt ... combines within himself ... a trained and well-informed scientist ... a Christian, who stands firmly in the tradition of historic Christianity ... (and) a human being, with all the personal vulnerability which this entails. (His) personal integrity shines through his book from beginning to end.*'

FROM THE FOREWORD BY JOHN STOTT
Rector Emeritus of All Souls, Langham Place, London, and President of the Institute of Contemporary Christianity

256 pages   *Paperback*

Inter-Varsity Press

Fertility and Faith

BRENDAN MCCARTHY

How should we regard fertility treatments?
What is the status of the embryo?
Is embryo research acceptable?

While research into techniques of human fertilization and embryology progresses rapidly, critical moral questions like these have yet to be answered. Churches have failed to influence the debate because of their incomplete understanding of the issues. Divergent views have lessened the impact of their response and have sent confusing messages to the rest of the world.

In his thorough and original analysis, Brendan McCarthy highlights the unclear moral basis of laws governing human fertilization techniques, and establishes a convincing foundation for a Christian approach.

Brendan McCarthy is a pastor of a community church in Northern Ireland. After their first two children died at birth due to a rare medical condition, he and his wife began to investigate fertility treatments and faced the question of which, if any, were compatible with their faith. This book grew out of that initial research.

288 pages

Paperback

Inter-Varsity Press

Taming your Emotional Tigers

TONY WARD

Loneliness, fear, failure, anger, depression, guilt.

Wild animals of emotion inhabit each of us. At best they cause discomfort; at worst they tear us apart. Can we ever hope to control them?

Tony Ward believes we can. Indeed, we must take responsibility for our own passions. It may be a long and gradual process but we do not need to surrender to them. This book shows us how we can begin to tame these emotional tigers under the gentle influence of the Holy Spirit.

'*A jewel of a book. Down to earth, insightful and thoroughly biblical. I intend to recommend it wherever I go.*'

SELWYN HUGHES
Crusade for World Revival

'*Tony Ward's book will stimulate and challenge you to rethink the way you live and renew your walk with God. A practical and pastoral book written sensitively for those who struggle with hurt feelings.*'

RUSS PARKER
Director, Acorn Christian Healing Trust

160 pages   *Paperback*

Inter-Varsity Press